FRIENDS of ~~the~~

FRIENDS
— *of a* —
LIFETIME

The Nun, the Infidel and the Superman

FELICITAS CORRIGAN

Collins

FOUNT PAPERBACKS

William Collins Sons & Co. Ltd
London · Glasgow · Sydney · Auckland
Toronto · Johannesburg

First published in 1985 by John Murray (Publishers) Ltd, London
This edition first published in Great Britain in 1990 by
Fount Paperbacks
Fount Paperbacks is an imprint of
Collins Religious Division,
part of the Collins Publishing Group
8 Grafton Street, London W1X 3LA

The play 'The Best of Friends' by Hugh Whitemore
is based on the correspondence between George B. Shaw,
Sydney Cockerell and Dame Laurentia McLachlan.

CONDITIONS OF SALE

Contents

Dedication

To the Stanbrook Community
past, present and to come
in the year of
Centenary & Jubilee
1984

Introductory Note

THIS BOOK, suggested by Mr John Murray, stems from the chapters in *In A Great Tradition* (1956, out of print for many years), dealing with the relationships of Dame Laurentia McLachlan with Bernard Shaw, Sir Sydney Cockerell and others. During the intervening years, not only has fresh material come to light—including a number of letters from Dame Laurentia to Bernard Shaw—but the climate of thought has altered. A good deal of new matter has been incorporated in the text, and anonymity everywhere dropped. Yet it is doubtful whether, in a monastic house like ours, any one member could make a Coriolanus-like boast of 'Alone I did it.' Such is the wholesome and wholesale traffic of minds, the generous sharing of skills and resources, that anything worthwhile is almost certainly born of collective effort. For that reason I should like to place on record my own indebtedness thirty years ago to Dame Scholastica Hebgin whose memory, to use the medieval phrase, 'abides in pleasantness and blessing'; to Dame Bede Foord my sometime fellow-novice, who compiled the index; and to Dame Margaret Truran, of the present happy band of youth, who has had a not inconsiderable hand in the production of this book. She found the warp of the opening chapter already set up, but by skilful selection of coloured threads from here, there and everywhere, has cunningly woven a differently-patterned weft.

Finally I wish to express my thanks to Michael Redington for personal encouragement and help, to the British Library for their help in making available copies of Dame Laurentia's letters to Bernard Shaw in their possession, and to the Public Trustee and the Society of Authors for permission to quote them.

D.F.C. 1984

Preface

THE LIFE, the influence and the friendships of the Benedictine nun, Dame Laurentia Margaret McLachlan, abbess of Stanbrook Abbey, Worcester, may seem something of an enigma to those who think of her life only in terms of the strict enclosure, high surrounding walls, grilles in church and parlour, and the locked and bolted doors demanded by the reforms of the Council of Trent (1545–63) and scrupulously observed until the Second Vatican Council, exactly four hundred years later. Had a woman of her calibre been a member of a far-flung modern congregation, her duties would doubtless have taken her to the ends of the earth, but the daily life of a strictly enclosed nun, however romantic to the imagination of a casual observer, offers little that is exciting or dramatic—six hours a day in her stall in choir, two or more hours of manual work in field or house, reading, study, the companionship of the same familiar circle. It is a life spent in hammering out within the silent factory of the cloister, benefits that are imponderable but priceless. The phrase has been taken straight out of Patrick Leigh Fermor's *A Time To Keep Silence*—that record of the intrepid traveller who dared to penetrate into the fastnesses of Benedictine strongholds, in order to find in a quiet cell the healing, peace and renewed vigour that he sought. In a passage admirable for its spiritual penetration, he sums up the essential strength of the life he found there, and its secret as a source of vitality both for those within and those without:

'Worship and prayer are the *raison d'être* of the Benedictine Order; and anything else, even their great achievements as scholars and architects and doctors of the church, is subsidiary.

1

They were, however, for centuries the only guardians of
literature, the classics, scholarship and the humanities in a
world of which the confusion can best be compared to our own
atomic era. For a long period, after the great epoch of Benedictine scholarship at Cluny, the Maurist Benedictine Abbey
of St Germain-des-Prés was the most important residuary of
learning and science in Europe. Only a few ivy-clad ruins
remain, just visible between *zazou* suits and existentialist
haircuts from the terrace of the *Deux Magots*. But in scores
of abbeys all over Europe, the same liberal traditions survive
and prosper. Other by-products of their life were the beautiful
buildings in which I was living, and the unparalleled calm
that prevailed there. At St Wandrille I was inhabiting at last
a tower of solid ivory, and I, not the monks, was the escapist.
For my hosts, the Abbey was a springboard into eternity; for
me a retiring place to write a book and spring more effectively
back into the maelstrom. Strange that the same habitat should
prove favourable to ambitions so glaringly opposed.'[1]

If, as Patrick Leigh Fermor asserts, worship, prayer and
scholarship are the criteria, then Dame Laurentia was a typical
Benedictine: her life-work was essentially the praise of God
through the solemnization of Mass and the liturgical Hours. Yet
her life itself was in some ways not typical, inasmuch as her
activities brought her by seemingly fortuitous circumstances into
contacts with movements and people normally outside the rather
circumscribed range of an enclosed nun. Whereas the tasks
assigned to her sprang from the very ethos of the life—music,
monastic history and liturgy—accidents of time and place gave
her a position of greater importance and influence than she
might otherwise have possessed.

Margaret McLachlan was born at Coatbridge, Lanarkshire, on
11 January 1866, the youngest of seven children. 'My father,
Henry McLachlan, was a brilliant, witty and handsome man,'
she wrote to a friend:

'I think most of his gaiety and charm must have come from

[1] *A Time to Keep Silence* by Patrick Leigh Fermor, p. 35 (John
Murray).

2

his mother, who was French. My mother, Mary McAleese, of a Northern Ireland family, was small, quiet, the sweetest, most self-effacing person in the world, yet she ruled an adoring husband and independent children, and made just the right balance for my father with his dash of French vivacity. My father revelled in all his children, but I am bound to say that his chief favourite was the youngest who was always with him when he was at home, and generally at his side when he drove about his public business in the highest dog-cart in the County. He could not bear life without a girl in the house and was miserable when, after failure of governesses, we three were sent to school (my elder sister and I to Edinburgh, the eldest to Stanbrook). I was recalled after a couple of terms and, under the plea, quite justified, of delicacy, had a glorious time with my father and brothers. A kind of intermittent education went on with my clerical brother as pedagogue. In 1879 I went to a Convent day-school and the next year as a boarder, and learned nothing. Then on September 5, 1881, I came here, had two years of excellent schooling, six months at home, and back here, for good.'

She was a precocious child, able to read and write long before she was given any explicit instruction; at six years of age she had a regular circle of correspondents. 'My time is not my own,' she informed one of them. Then, anxious to avoid the hackneyed phrase, she altered her usual preamble from 'I was very glad to get your letter' to 'I received your letter with the greatest animosity.' When, however, the halcyon days of childhood and freedom came to an end, it was a small, rebellious, woebegone girl of fifteen who was admitted to the Stanbrook school on 5 September 1881. On the same date, only three years later, she was clothed in the religious habit of a Benedictine novice.

'Had I the choice again as a young girl,' she wrote, 'I should most certainly repeat my life. I sometimes marvel at my wisdom in making the choice, for I was young and fairly foolish and terribly fond of pleasure.' Only once in her life did she leave the shores of England. At seventeen, she travelled to Solesmes with Dom Laurence Shepherd to spend some weeks at Ste Cécile, while he visited his close friend Dom Prosper Guéranger, abbot of St Pierre. They paused at Chartres on the way—a fleeting visit that left on her an indelible mark. Externally there is little more to say. How then could she have built up such deep and abiding friendships, not only with those of her own faith, but with men such as Sydney C. Cockerell and George Bernard Shaw?

To appreciate this one must understand something of the setting in which she grew up and developed, the people among whom she lived, and the tradition they had inherited and strengthened. The influence of tradition, educative and restraining, is necessary in any culture or in any well-rooted family life. But whereas in a family it may be snapped in a single generation, that of a long-established religious house is something far more formidable, intense and tenacious. It is not merely a matter of distinctive dress, exacting ceremonial, and a code of etiquette laboriously acquired; it is something deeper, less definable, only gradually apprehended and absorbed, yet a powerful element in the very life-stream. The only thing to compare with it, however remotely, is the carefully cherished spirit of some ancient school or university. This is especially true of England where, from the seventh century to the present day, Benedictines have left a mark on the life, laws, institutions and character of the people not easily obliterated. It betrays itself not only in affection for liturgical functions apparent, for instance, in the stately rites of the Church of England and in the ceremonial of Parliament, not only in the ancient universities, whose wide-sleeved black gown is suspiciously reminiscent of the Benedictine cowl worn in choir, but even more significantly in a sobriety of judgement, a temper of mind reflective rather than speculative, and in a love of law and order. It cannot be said that Dame Laurentia was simply a product of the Rule of St Benedict and her own house; yet without them she would not have been all that she was.

In 1907, a few weeks after their first meeting, Sydney Cockerell, writing to Dame Laurentia from Newbuildings, home of Wilfrid Scawen Blunt, observed in his postscript that the old house formerly belonged to a well-known Catholic family, the Carylls. She immediately told him of the special interest the Carylls had for Stanbrook, since Dom Alexius Caryll had been chaplain to the community at Cambray in 1669. In his next letter S.C.C. asked her correct title, and added two sizeable queries—how recently was the community at Cambray, and how did she acquire her scholarship? Her reply packs three hundred years into a neat summary:

'Our community was founded at Cambray in 1625 by the English monks, then recently formed into a Congregation. They, as you know, come down in a direct line from the old English Black Monks, but the nuns have no such claim with regard to the earlier times. Our house is of course entirely English. The foundress, Dame Gertrude More, was great-great-granddaughter of Sir Thomas More. We remained at Cambray till 1793, when we were taken away by force (with only half an hour's notice) and carried off in open carts to Compiègne. There the nuns (21 in number) were detained for 18 months in a miserable prison, and three died of the hardships and privations. The survivors expected nothing but the guillotine, but the death of Robespierre set them free. They returned to England in great poverty, and were for a short time in Lancashire. Then the Hall at Abbots Salford was kindly lent to them for some years and finally, in 1838, they acquired this property, built a chapel, and added to the Hall. The new Church was built in 1871, and the Monastery was begun a few years later; it is still unfinished.

'What am I to say about the sources of what you are pleased to call "my scholarship"? St Benedict's daughters have a traditional love of study, though they like to keep quiet and hidden and leave the more public part to their brethren. In our community there is a strong liturgical tradition, which is natural considering the important place the Choir plays in our daily life. The little knowledge I possess has been gained in the course of my "religious life", as we call it. From the beginnings of the movement for restoring the original Plainsong we have been interested and, as we use the mediaeval version daily, we have of course, studied the matter pretty thoroughly.

'From the time of our foundation our nuns have been called *Dame*, but we call ourselves "Sister". The form of address is: Dame Laurentia McLachlan, O.S.B. The title corresponds to the monks' Dan or Dom.'

Begging her to ignore his questions if they seemed impertinent, he plunged straight in:

'Did you leave the world because you thought it a wicked place and to save your own soul? or because thus shielded from much that is evil as well as from much that is good, you felt that you could better obey the precepts of Christ and live in a manner more pleasing to God than your life would otherwise have been? If these are impertinent questions, of course you will ignore them. They are not intended to be so, and if you care to ask me any in return I will gladly answer. I cannot quite divest myself of the feeling that good women and women of valiant natures who withdraw from the battle come under Dante's condemnation, when he talks of someone as having been guilty of *il gran rifiuto*—words which Ruskin said were always dinning in his ears. I myself as a mere camp-follower and despoiler of the slain come surely under the same ban—but then I was always a skulker, loving my ease—which is not the case with you.'

Queries such as these could have afforded an excellent opportunity for a display of heroics. Rhetoric and fine-sounding phrases, however, were not her style, and her unassuming reply strives after no effect:

'If I thought you put these questions in a spirit of mere curiosity, I should ignore them; but I know that is not the case, so I answer them in the spirit in which you ask them. I had no fault to find with the world as I knew it, and home was heaven. In leaving the world the motives you mention (desire of giving one's undivided service to God and of following the Gospel counsels as well as the precepts) were of course at the bottom, but it would be difficult to explain exactly what was the spring of one's action. A vocation—any kind of vocation—is a very personal matter, a very real thing too, though so impalpable, and its effects are very enduring. It is in fact the whole secret of our life. There is no idea of getting out of the battle of life (if that were possible), and I don't feel that I in any way wronged the world by leaving it! Of course we consider that we have very serious obligations towards the world, the chief of which is prayer for those we have left behind, and for all in general. I wonder how much you believe in prayer?

'The religious name depends on many things—personal devotion, or special suitableness, or local reasons, or the abbess's choice. Some people keep their baptismal names. St Laurence the Martyr is my patron, and a grand inspiring one too. The name was chosen for me as there was and is great devotion to the Saint at Stanbrook, and they wanted a Laurentia.'

Her correspondent did not deny that he preferred her baptismal saint. 'I am so glad that you really are a Margaret,' he told her. 'A dragon is such a more attractive companion than a gridiron: and I wonder that you were not afraid of vexing St Margaret when you cast off her name. Besides, there are pretty associations with pearls & daisies.' He had just acquired and was to give Dame Laurentia a copy of G. G. Coulton's rendering of *Pearl*, the exquisite 14th-century lament of a father over the grave of his infant daughter Margaret, with his sudden recognition of her in a Beatrice-like vision:

> 'O Spotless Pearl in pearls so pure,
> Thou bearest,' quoth I, 'the Pearl of Price!'

But the Kalendar of Saints has seventeen Margarets, and S.C.C. was confusing Dame Laurentia's Scottish patroness with the third century Margaret of Antioch, killed by the sword, and enormously popular throughout the Middle Ages, as witnessed by her frequent appearance trampling on the dragon in illumination, painting and sculpture, to say nothing of her admonitions to Joan of Arc. Dame Laurentia's smiling non-committal 'I am glad my name is of satisfaction to you' was guaranteed to offend neither of the two Saints.

In these days when we hear much of vocational guidance, her use of the term 'vocation' may be misleading unless understood as that specific call from God, known only to those who receive it. Some people may deplore that such a personality as Dame

Laurentia should have been lost to a world where she might have exercised an even wider and more beneficial influence. If so, they fail to recognize that it was precisely this vocation and discipline which made her what she was, and enabled her to do what she did. It is the old paradox of fulfilment through renunciation for Christ's sake—*cui servire regnare est*—of the life freely given and the hundredfold received. After a cordial friendship that enjoyed sunshine and survived storm, Bernard Shaw was to address her with patent sincerity as a woman without frontiers, one of the few people who really mattered to him for, he assured her, 'though you are an enclosed nun you do not have an enclosed mind, as so many women at large have.' That victory lay with the nun behind bars was proved beyond doubt when the unyielding Sydney Cockerell finally conceded, 'I am not prepared to say that your choice was not the right one. Indeed I regard you as a beacon from which spread shafts of all the virtues to lighten those who sit in darkness—or as a piece of radium which can heal and strengthen those who falter, without losing any of its own substance.'

1

The Friend

'As to the effect of our life, I think no outsider can realize how it deepens the sense of human solidarity and fellowship—with the world at large. You know St Benedict had a vision in which he saw the whole world in a sunbeam. That of course is only an attempt at describing what is indescribable, but it may convey to you something of what I mean. Striving for nearness to God, one gets to look at things in Him and as we may believe He sees them. That makes one interested in every kind of person and work in a way that I am sure I should never have been had I remained in the world.'

THOSE WORDS were written in 1922, when Dame Laurentia had been thirty-eight years a nun and Subprioress for twelve years; in three years she would be Prioress and six years later Abbess. For nearly fifty years, through her great gifts, she was the vital force in the community, utterly loyal to her abbess—indeed for many years her chief support. God seemed to have given to her, as he gave to Solomon, 'wisdom and understanding exceeding much, and largeness of heart as the sand that is on the sea shore.' Far from destroying, grace spiritualized her natural qualities, and as a consequence of her ability to enter into the human heart by her power of sympathy and affection, she exerted an astonishing influence over a large and varied circle of friends. 'In her own inimitable way,' wrote one of her friends, 'she gave herself to every one who sought her help; she was a person without frontiers. It often seems to me that one of God's gifts to those who renounce everything for Him is a greater sense of union with all men, a greater power to help, and a deeper charity than anything known in the world. Hers was the spirit of St Benedict radiating outwards, and how many souls through her and through the whole being of the Abbey were brought nearer to God.'

This woman 'without frontiers' could count among her friends dignitaries of the Catholic Church and leading figures of the Church of England, scholars ardently Catholic and openly agnostic, men and women devoted to the drama and the stage, poets, parents, craftsmen, humble labourers—they crowd in a richly varied and diverting procession. It is rare to find a human being who attracts equally men and women, old and young as she undoubtedly did.

The secret lay in Dame Laurentia's ability to give to the utmost, and that in turn was rooted in her wholehearted dedication to whatever her monastic vocation might entail. With her varied gifts of mind and character she threw herself first and foremost into every activity likely to increase the happiness of the community. Her letters abound in references to events of daily life, the morning call, industries and recreations, the cycle of festivities: all bear eloquent witness to her own verve and driving force. The writer who acknowledged an Easter letter in the following manner can never have been a dull companion:

'It was a great pleasure to have your Easter greetings, for one likes to feel one's best friend near at that beautiful time. For us here it is a bit of heaven, and everything was in tune this year, the community well and vigorous, the weather lovely and the birds beyond praising. I am having my annual rapture at the return of spring. It begins on the first morning that I am awakened by a bird's song. This year a blackbird has taken upon itself the office of calling me, and it makes me fresh at once. Thrushes used to be my favourite song-birds, but I am now fonder of the blackbird,—at least I think I am. That lazy, meditative whistle is so expressive.'

She loved the birds that found sanctuary from a noisy world within the old high-walled garden. Year after year she derived entertainment from the domestic affairs of the colony of rooks, vigilant watchmen against invading hawk or kestrel from their points of vantage in the sentinel elm and chestnut trees. Or she would follow with amusement the ridiculous games played nightly by the screaming contingent of blackbirds and thrushes in hot pursuit of her favourite brown owl as he flew from tree to tree. Her chosen spot during the summer months was down by the fish-pond with its hint of

> *thrilling-sweet and rotten*
> *Unforgettable, unforgotten*
> *River-smell.*

Here she would watch the swallows come to give their display of delirious evolutions over the water and chatter in charming conversation from the willows, or the cock-linnet, with his splash of crimson, perching on a golden water-lily and swaying gently in an effort to drink. She would observe with special delight the nest of grey-green eggs laid by the moorhens, Stanbrook's heraldic birds, among the willow roots, and wait for the appearance of the smoke-black balls of fluff that in due course would emerge from the herbage.

'Our birds are extraordinarily tame. The chaffinches almost get under our feet and even thrushes and blackbirds are not shy. Of course the robins are great friends, and at least one of them seems to know how to read! At any rate this is a true story. A robin had frequented the printing house all winter, and a box of crumbs was kept for his use. I found that his visits seriously interfered with the work of some of the young compositors, and hardening my heart I told the head printer that no feeding must be done during work-hours. She put up a notice to that effect. Next day in comes the robin, perches as usual on a case and sings for his breakfast. No response. He looks about greatly mystified, then hops round the room and arrives before the notice,—reads it carefully, and hops off to the crumb box, which has been left open, helps himself and flies out without saying a word. For the rest of the winter he observed the same monastic custom!'

Dame Laurentia never gave the impression of being a rigid ascetic: quite the contrary. But possibly the fact that she was so full of joy is itself a proof that she had trodden hard ways. In that admirably terse way of hers, she once summed up the main trials of the religious life. To a friend who evidently accused her of 'escapism' she wrote:

'You do not think—do you?—that in religious life one avoids thorns and thistles. To begin with, seventy people cannot live together without occasional sparks being struck out. Then the ordeals of an earnest spiritual life are very searching. Besides that, communities often have severe trials of one sort or another. I don't wish to make you believe that we are the most deeply afflicted people on earth—only to remark that one does not get out of troubles by leaving the world. For my own part I think it would be immoral if we did, for why should we have such a blessed life for nothing?'

The counsel she invariably gave in the face of tribulation sprang from deep conviction born of experience: 'trust in God and in each other.' That this was a guiding principle became clear in the address given to the community in 1931, following her election as Abbess, when she quoted the remark of a newly ordained bishop, '"I have heard the truth for the last time," meaning that henceforth he would be flattered, or perhaps only half-informed. There should be nothing of that between us; the Abbess should be able to hear freely and able to speak freely.' From the outset it was plain her position as superior in no way impaired the friendship that had always marked her easy relations with her monastic family. Awkwardness was soon forgotten. Barely a fortnight after that first abbatial address, Dame Anne Dowson was writing to Sydney Cockerell:

'My emotions have been very mixed of late. Naturally I hoped she would be elected for large reasons; for myself I felt it was utter desolation. I had, through those months of her illness, got to know her so much better and, I think she would allow me to say it, I had found a friend, one to whom I talked without ceremony. . . . And at first I thought I cannot possibly be at ease with someone who wears a large gold cross on her chest; I seemed to see nothing else. However, she saw my state and has pulled me out of it. Though I have lost many things that can never come again, I have not lost my friend.'

Those who knew her best belonged to her own community, but inevitably her gift for friendship is best observed in her relationships outside her immediate monastic family. 'What a mystery friendship is!' she once wrote. 'One of those subtle and beautiful forces that glorify life. And how strangely and delightfully different one's friends are one from the other—not only in themselves, but in the way one has to look at them. Some we have to carry, while others carry us. The perfect friend, to my mind, is one who believes in one once and for all, and never requires explanations and assurances. But I did not start out to write a treatise *De amicitia*.' Independent and forceful leader that she was, she did not readily look for or accept the help of others. It is possibly an over-simplification, but it would seem not improbable that in her long religious life there were only two or three people, apart from her Abbess, upon whose guidance she really leaned: Dom Aidan Gasquet, Conventual Prior of Downside 1878 to 1884 and Cardinal 1914 to 1929; Dr Thomas Williams, Archbishop of Birmingham from 1929 to 1946, and Dr Finbar Ryan OP, Archbishop of Port-of-Spain from 1940 to 1966.

Gasquet the historian has had a bad press from both G. G. Coulton and David Knowles. Behind the historian, and entirely unsuspected by the world at large, was a side of his nature which he showed to those under his protection, from nuns to seminarians, a delicacy and charm of manner which inspired affection and gratitude, a 'gentleness and constant thought for others'.

His frequent visits were always acclaimed: he knew every nun in the house and often appealed for help in his many tasks. One typed his manuscripts, another compiled his indices, others were engaged in printing his apologia *Religio Religiosi* or some other work born of his enthusiasm. During an outbreak of tuberculosis which robbed the house of many young nuns—in 1910 no fewer than four died—nothing could have surpassed Abbot Gasquet's kindness. If at all possible, he would slip away from his many duties to spend the weekend at Stanbrook, often pontificating at ceremonies in order to give pleasure and distract the community from their anxiety concerning the invalids. He made practical provisions for the welfare of all, tempering the somewhat too austere regime, adjusting the timetable to prolong slightly the time allotted to rest, and in countless ways showing a truly fatherly solicitude that was combined with great courtesy and tact. 'I think this year,' he wrote early in 1910 to the new Sub-prioress, 'the strain on all has been so much that the usual Lent fast should be mitigated. . . . I have told the Abbess so, so please back me up.'

By temperament, personality and community of interest, it was Dame Laurentia who was on closest terms with him. She was not blind to his failings as a scholar, his inaccuracy and his tendency, where his was no more than the original idea, to take the credit for the actual work done by others. When in 1919 the Abbey press printed the first volume of *The Letters of St Teresa*, bearing an introduction by Cardinal Gasquet, Sydney Cockerell commented, 'The Cardinal's introduction seems to have been written half by Newman and the other half by the learned editress of the volume, though this is an inference.' Back came a reply of typical honesty. 'You are very severe on the Cardinal! All the same your inference is perfectly correct.' Whatever his weaknesses, his infectious enthusiasm for historical research, his flair for discovering an important manuscript, his readiness to discuss and guide the studies of others were of paramount importance during Dame Laurentia's early and formative monastic years. It is true to say that, without him, she would not have become the scholar she did. Her letters abound in appreciative references to him, to his constant encouragement and generous praise, and also to the wisdom of his spiritual teaching. The admiration and affection were mutual. 'Dame Laurentia has more insight into the human soul,' he once declared, 'than anyone, man or woman, I have ever known.'

Her surviving letters testify to a myriad of monastic correspondents and to a continuum of friendship with all the English Benedictine houses. In her seventy years at Stanbrook she witnessed the history of the Congregation in its making and had vital contacts with most of the makers. 'She was almost a "Mother" to all of us in the Congregation, interested in all that concerned its welfare, wise in counsel, and learned too,' wrote Abbot Christopher Butler of Downside. Her advice and musical expertise were constantly in demand as each house in turn adopted the 'restored' style of plainsong: lengthy questions came, *inter alios*, from Dom Cuthbert Butler, Dom Roger Hudleston and Dom Alphege Shebbeare of Downside, Dom Clement Sherlock of Douai and Dom Dunstan Sibley of Belmont.

Two friendships were especially dear to her: those with the Master of St Benet's Hall, Oxford, Dom Justin McCann of Ampleforth, 'my best monk-friend' as Dame Laurentia described him when he acted as deacon at her abbatial blessing; and with the Abbot of Downside, Dom Cuthbert Butler. The latter had first come to Stanbrook in 1885 and repeated his visit almost every year thereafter till his death in 1933. With him would come the script of whatever he was working on; he would read parts aloud to the community and then expect comments. Knowing everyone in the house, he 'took a great interest in all our doings', Dame Laurentia acknowledged; it was through him that her article on the so-called 'Portiforium Oswaldi' was published by the *Journal of Theological Studies* in 1929. Once, when sections of her great work on the Worcester Antiphoner were being published, she admitted disappointment that her work was always swallowed 'without the compliment of enquiry'. Abbot Butler, present at the time, apparently comforted her with the tale of his *Lausiac History*; after years of work it finally appeared in print, but the *Downside Review* had to beg him to review it himself.

Abbesses of Benedictine houses on the Continent as well as in England were her friends; the Prioress of Parramatta in Australia found her an unfailing confidant. Above all she showered affection on the house of Santa Maria in São Paulo, Brazil, whose foundresses had been trained at Stanbrook, and the house of Santa Escolastica in Buenos Aires that sprang from it. The frequent letters to their 'dearest Grandmother' from the flourishing community of young nuns in Argentina, brimful of enthusiasm for monastic tradition, were a source of immense interest and delight to Dame Laurentia during her last years, and on her part she did all in her power to help and encourage their youthful Abbess in the first and difficult years of the foundation.

Her sympathies were not confined to members of her own Order. Nuns of many kinds sought her guidance and occasionally had reason to thank her for possibly saving their vocations. She could use the surgeon's knife, when necessary, with relentless kindness. And in the world outside the cloister Dame Laurentia followed the spiritual progress of many women with close concern and attention. To Yseulte Mitford, who had recently tried her vocation at Stanbrook, she found time to write a letter whose contents, from everyday news of monastic life to firm guidance along a quite different path, must have gone far to dispel feelings of rejection and regret.

Candlemas 1910

'All these feasts remind me so of you, and I know they will make you sad, but have courage, my dear Yseulte, and do not give way to regrets. I understand what you say about facing life with joy. It is a great secret, but the lesson is not an easy one to learn. One has to labour to get the centre of one's joy placed in the supernatural and firmly anchored there. You know the beautiful text: "The joy of the Lord is our strength." I wish you this strength, which gives a new meaning to life by forcing us to rejoice *in the Lord* even when one feels inclined to be sad and discouraged. Joy is a beautiful, unselfish virtue.'

Limned in bold strokes in a series of lively letters to Sydney Cockerell is the portrait of 'my "son" Joe', alias Miriam Filose, whose short time on earth in all its varying fortunes she guided with the greatest affection. 'A born soldier, the product of a race of soldiers,' 'Joe' came of a Greek family which had settled in Naples, and later in India where her father, Colonel Filose, was on the staff of the Maharajah of Gwalior. The letters throw a vivid light on Dame Laurentia's predilection for tomboys and her sympathy with women's determined bid for equality during the First World War.

'I am watching with the greatest interest the social changes in the country, and especially the development of woman's sphere. I am fortunate in being in close touch with typical women of various kinds, and they interest me enormously. I have among my "spiritual children" a boy-girl of the latest type. . . . She is a splendid girl, so wholesome and downright and so strong. A few weeks ago when she was looking round the church at Ludlow in her full uniform, the charwoman came up and said sternly: "If you were a gentleman you would take off your cap!"'

Some time later she encloses a letter with the comment:

'Here is a letter from my boy-girl who is an ambulance driver in France—such a character! She was a wild jungle child in her young days and is still a delightful savage—a kind of "Kim". She was in Italy for nearly a year—and in the last Italian push, and is now at Etaples. . . . She is a most extraordinary mixture, [Dame Laurentia continued in her next letter] twenty-six years of age but will not grow up. . . . Lots of brains, especially musical ones, a heart of gold, quite unconventional, so that she is always shocking people and giving quite the wrong impression of herself till they know her. She was sent to me to be tamed five years ago. The process took some time and trouble, but she is now the most obedient (to me) girl in the world, though still nice and wild. She has a passion for helping lame dogs over stiles and is always getting herself into the funniest situations.'

The situation was far from being funny when the girl was involved in a serious outbreak of fire a few weeks later in which everything she possessed at the time was destroyed, she herself narrowly escaping with her life. As soon as she was free she made her way to Stanbrook: 'Joe turned up here as follows: her own long boots, a deceased Tommy's breeches, overcoat (with A.S.C. "numerals") and cap, a Women's Legion tunic borrowed from her sister, a haversack, and *praeterea nihil*! She really *was* a boy this time.'

The ways and means she took to tame the turbulent spirit of the girl called to sanctity have remained Dame Laurentia's own secret. Before her death she made a bonfire of letters which in her opinion no eyes but her own should read; all records of her course of spiritual *ascesis* have consequently perished. Another, however, the writer and calligrapher Christopher St John, cherished with especial tenderness by reason of the tragic background of her childhood, has told of her close and intimate relationship with the nun who became to her more than a mother:

'In 1909–1910 when I lived in Rome, and became an ardent practising Catholic, I met Miss Ethel Ruxton who never tired of singing the praises of Stanbrook. If her health had allowed she would have tried her vocation there.—"You must know Dame Laurentia, she is the most wonderful woman I have ever known." Miss Ruxton or "Dully", as Dame Laurentia called her, took me to Stanbrook on August 2, 1910, and at first sight I loved Dame Laurentia and trusted her. . . . In October 1910 I spent a week at Callow End and saw her every day. She gave me instruction in the liturgy, put me on the right lines in prayer, in every way increased my love for Christ and His Church. I had never been so well understood by anyone. I never found a "spiritual adviser" in a priest, but I found one in her.

'I think in the early days she thought I might find my vocation in the religious life. "You have one characteristic that would help you," she said laughing, "docility". This surprised me very much, as I had not got that reputation in the world. Well, though I was quite convinced that monks and nuns choose the better part, I felt, perhaps wrongly, that the choice was beyond me. Dame Laurentia never showed the slightest disappointment over this.

'I cannot go into all the incidents of our friendship, but let me recall that when Abbess Caecilia and Dame Laurentia went on a mission to a Benedictine house[1] in Wales (converts at the same time as the Caldey monks) to put the nuns on the right lines, I had the privilege of meeting them at Cardiff on their way home and travelled with them to Worcester. I was much struck by their calm and dignity in their unaccustomed surroundings. When I read books like *I Leap Over the Wall* in which ex-nuns say how bewildered they are when they go back to the world, I remember how much less flustered my charges were at stations than ordinary travellers.'

Dame Laurentia was accustomed to say that God would work a miracle or send one of his angels in order to help a soul in real need. She could not work miracles, but she could and did do much to help others. Once being asked by a correspondent for direction

[1] Milford Haven, now Talacre Abbey.

to assist at Mass and receive Holy Communion in as perfect dispositions as possible, she jotted down on some sheets of ordinary notepaper concise doctrinal and liturgical notes which in their complete freedom from pious jargon are admirable illustrations of the clarity and virility which invariably marked her advice. They are too long to be quoted here, but the same force and economy of words characterize her advice in the following letter written to Christopher St John in September 1935.

'With regard to your two queries. . . . The danger of abusing the confessional is not difficult to deal with. Anything may be abused but in this case the disadvantages are far outbalanced by good effects.--Your other point—it is not necessary to perfect forgiveness to cease to feel that the injury done *was* an injury and injustice. Truth cannot be denied. What we have to do is to banish all resentment and try to keep our minds off the grievance, for it is sure to keep recurring to our minds.'

If, however, rebuke were needed, rebuke followed. Some years later Christopher St John sent Dame Laurentia a rather severe criticism of Victoria Sackville-West's *The Eagle and the Dove*. The reply is typical of the writer's extraordinary generosity towards those not usually associated in the public mind with spiritual matters.

12.*xi*.43

'*The Eagle and the Dove* came after your letter and I have only just finished it. I find it for the most part *excellent* which, I am told, is Father Steuart's word for it. In her appreciation of the great St Teresa I find nothing amiss; on the contrary, an amazing understanding and a balanced judgement. The little Saint seems to me less happily handled. The Saint's environment and education is repellent to most of us, and the sentimentality of her style revolts those who cannot see the strength it hides. All the same this second part is very interesting and I marvel that one who has not the faith can be so sympathetic. The passages about spiritual desolation (in the Dove) are the only pieces that jar. I suspect that you were referring to these in your letter. The love of God for man and of man for God cannot be judged or regulated by natural standards.'

This appreciation and approval of Vita Sackville-West's portrait of St Teresa of Avila is doubly interesting, coming as it does from one who was herself repeatedly likened to the great Carmelite. Those who came to see Dame Laurentia almost always wanted others to meet her in order to share the happiness of knowing her. 'All my friends who have been with me to Stanbrook,' writes one who knew her well, 'have soon got over their shyness of the grille. "She makes one feel it is less of a barrier than many barriers in the world." Her charm, her delicious sense of humour made them feel at ease. I doubt if any nun (except perhaps St Teresa of Avila) has ever been more gay.' She certainly had something of St Teresa's sparkling wit and power of communicating her own deep Christian joy. Many an anecdote might be related by way of illustration: one must suffice.

Madame de Navarro who, as Mary Anderson the beautiful American actress, had once taken England by storm during her short and brilliant career on the stage, was a near neighbour at Broadway. On her frequent visits to Stanbrook she became intimately acquainted with Dame Laurentia. She used often to recall in later years an amusing incident in the early days of their friendship. Eager to teach the *Salve Regina* to the country choir of the little church at Broadway, she sought Dame Laurentia's advice as to its interpretation. The latter asked her to sing it. Had the performance been given in the London Lyceum it would have evoked thunderous applause. As it was her solitary auditor gave vent to an agonized cry of: "Oh, Mary, don't! You can't sing to God like *that*"—uttered in tones of such mingled amusement and despair that the abashed performer declared they would ring in her ears until her dying day.

During the First World War Madame de Navarro occasionally returned to the stage in aid of war charities. In 1916, again meeting Ellen Terry, an old friend of hers, she invited her and her daughter, Edith Craig, to her home. She had long wanted to introduce Ellen Terry to Stanbrook and was not slow to seize the opportunity. On May 8 she wrote to Dame Laurentia:

'Dear Dame Laurentia,
    'It will be delightful to go to lunch with you on Sunday in company with that charming Nell Terry and Edy Craig. We

will be with you at 1. Today is the great day at Stratford—the performance begins at 1.30. I come on at about 4 o'clock. I have been appearing several times lately as Lady Macbeth, and Queen Hermione in *Winter's Tale*. Oh! I do wish you could have seen the glorious tribute to Shakespeare at Old Drury on Tuesday—but I will tell you all about it on Sunday.'

Two famous Shakespearian actresses, a reigning abbess and a future abbess deep in discussion of Shakespeare's plays on either side of a grille in a monastic parlour is not a subject for the conventional hagiographer. Possibly hagiography would benefit not a little if it sometimes were. What is striking, however, is the effect a bare room with a crucifix, a few chairs and a double iron grille for sole furniture had upon one who for sixty years was the idol of the theatre in two continents, and has gone down to posterity as one of the greatest actresses of her time: 'I shall never forget my happy day when my Edy and Mary Anderson brought me to see you,' wrote Ellen Terry afterwards on green notepaper in green ink to Dame Laurentia. 'It is a very great wish of mine that my little grandchild Nelly should have the privilege of seeing you and, if it were possible, of living at Stanbrook. I *know* what a happy-jolly life the child would have there—and what kindness and goodness she would meet with. A blessed happening devoutly to be wished—if only one's wishes could come true. . . .'

Not many people, least of all one accustomed to theatre dressing-rooms everlastingly laden with gifts and flowers, would envisage for a favourite grandchild 'a happy-jolly life' behind a grille; it is a significant tribute to the supernatural holiness, sincerity and gaiety of the two nuns, which an artist of Ellen Terry's calibre and a woman of Ellen Terry's humility and other-worldliness was quick to recognize. For years afterwards she recalled her visit to Stanbrook with enthusiastic delight. Her *Memoirs* quote a letter, finer than many a sermon on Christian charity and the duty of forgiveness, in which having reinforced a quotation from Shakespeare with a text from her beloved Thomas à Kempis, she goes on to express a desire to study St Thomas Aquinas. 'Talking of Tommy à K. I want those dear nuns at Stanbrook to tell me if I could learn from another Tommy, Thomas Aquinas,' she remarks naïvely. 'I believe he is immensely learned but very interesting. Dame Laurentia would know.'

There are so many other scenes and people one would like to recall: the delightful recreations spent in the large parlour with Mrs Gordon Woodhouse of Armscote, the famous harpsichordist, who used to bring over her charming little octavina, or in later days a specially designed clavichord, and give recitals of Bach and Scarlatti. She declared that Dame Laurentia was the most musical woman she had ever known; and her own knowledge of musicians was world-wide. Then there was Monsignor John O'Connor who with dreamy, abstracted air would entertain Abbess and community with his rambling, brilliant monologues, recounting, in his best Father Brown vein, tales of his adventures with G. K. Chesterton, telling ghost stories, or constructing a truly astonishing life-story of St Michael the Archangel from the New Testament. The Stanbrook library contains a volume of his poetry with the characteristic inscription: 'To Mother Laurentia from John O'Connor. In the blest assurance that if she can stand Barney Shaw, she can stand *him*.'

To enumerate all Dame Laurentia's friends is an impossible task, but it would convey an entirely false impression of her true self to imply that she only consorted with the great. On the contrary, she gave herself as completely and wholeheartedly to a child or the poorest labourer as to the most eminent scholar. With 'the darling young', indeed, she entered at once on a footing of equality and friendship. As Abbess she constantly came into contact with the small brothers and sisters, or nephews and nieces of the community. On one occasion she went to greet a two-year-old nephew of one of her nuns. Standing up to his full height on the counter at the other side of the grille, the small boy gazed somewhat coldly on the coloured woollen ball she held out as her token of friendship.

"No, thank you, Lady Abbess," he said in resolute tones, "I have one in my play-box."

Before his outraged parents could give vent to expressions of shocked annoyance, "That's right, David, perfectly right," she cried in tones of warmest approbation. "You'll be a monk some day. Never have two of a thing when one will do." And she forthwith departed, to return in a few moments with a gift better suited to his ripe years, and one which restored complete mutual understanding and respect. Or she could engender an atmosphere of domestic intimacy and easy familiarity by demonstrating the working of a toy sewing machine to two small girls, who watched her performance with spell-bound interest and departed with the treasure, convinced that of all her friends in the whole world, the Abbess of Stanbrook loved them by far the best.

One day Dame Laurentia received a very well-informed letter concerning St Egwin of Evesham which gave her the impression that the scholar who signed himself John Caine was at least a bearded F.S.A. She invited him to call for further discussion of the interesting points he had raised. He turned out to be a tall, grave young man who discoursed with a learned air about many archaeological points concerned with Evesham. In the course of conversation he alluded to his extreme youth, complaining that it was an obstacle to his approaching deans and chapters of cathedrals.

"Why, how old are you?" she asked.

"Eighteen, and you'd better call me John," was the reply.

He had just left Downside. She was delighted with this astounding boy with a remarkable flair for the right way to set about 'things archeological', as she later described him in a letter, and immediately informed him that she appointed him to succeed Sir Ivor Atkins and Stanbrook in matters Wigornian. By way of practical encouragement she straightway applied to the Dean and Chapter of Hereford Cathedral, who acceded to her request for the loan from their library of the thirteenth-century Passionale containing a life of St Ecgwine ("John insists on this spelling") and she then set about the task of procuring from Emmanuel College, Cambridge, the loan of a further manuscript necessary for the work of collation. At the time of this first meeting the Abbess was eighty-three years of age.

On another occasion, John Caine recalled in 1984, 'an extern sister came up after Benediction and said, "Lady Abbess would like to offer you some refreshment." There we sat in the large parlour, she on her side of the grate and me on mine, but I had also a tray with biscuits and a flagon of cider. "Help yourself," she said. I was polite and nervous in those days; I struggled with the stopper to the bottle, poured out my glass and politely sipped my cider and munched my biscuits as the talk went on—no doubt

about that exceedingly useful saint, Ecgwine. Eventually my glass
was empty. "Well, that was really nice," I thought. After a bit
she broke off, looked at the bottle and me in some apprehension,
"Aren't you going to finish the bottle?" she asked. "Men always
did when I was a girl."'

A few days after Dame Laurentia's death the F.S.A. wrote to
a friend in the community: "When you are as young and as
determinedly unimpressed as I was when I first met her, you do
not readily admit to deep impressions; but I remember thinking
as I went home after our first talk, "She must be one of the very
few people in life who matter."'

She occupied a large place in the life of another young man of
very different character and condition of life. An Italian workman
who gloried in the name of Crescenzo Malatesta arrived under
duress as a prisoner of war from a neighbouring camp, refused
repatriation at the close of hostilities, and begged to be allowed
to remain in the service of the community. For years he received
food, clothes, medicine and whatever else he needed from the
monastery, which became his home in a very real sense. 'We
have become, he says, his father, mother, brothers and sisters,'
Dame Laurentia commented. 'He is the merriest little soul from
the South and sings like Caruso over his work.' On the red-letter
days when his mother in Naples, 'la Signora Teresa', wrote to
him, the Abbess would herself go out to find him at work in the
garden, in order to deliver the letter and share his excitement
and pleasure. Amid her many responsibilities and cares she found
time to send regular bulletins to his parents, giving them reports
on their son's welfare. A letter to Sydney Cockerell in 1949, in
which she encloses an epistle written on magnificent gold-
bordered scalloped notepaper embossed with a Madonna, Bam-
bino and angel in rich hues of red, blue, green and yellow, relates
a delightful incident when her 'verray parfit gentil knight'
presented his lady with a gift worthy of her high station:

'You must make acquaintance with the writer of the enclosed
letter. He came to us as a prisoner-of-war three years ago after
eight or so years in the Italian army and he is our best farm-
labourer and absolutely devoted to the place. He has just been
home to Campo Basso [sic], near Naples, for the first time since

boyhood and has returned with joy. There are gifts of cheese
and fruit from Italy, and for me a gold ring which he presented
very shyly, wondering whether I would accept it—as if I
would think of refusing. It is quite good and fits me perfectly.
I think of wearing it in bed and often enough to exhibit it to
the good little man when I meet him in the grounds. He really
. . . has perfect manners. I correspond with his mother, who
would not believe until I assured her, that her son was working
in a "Convento". You will find a postscript from her at the
end of Malatesta's letter.'

The gold ring, adorned with a large initial R for Remem-
brance, was presented in a little oval pale-green box edged with
white, and ever afterwards occupied a place of honour among the
abbatial rings worn on feasts of varying solemnity.

Regarded for over half a century as the leading English
authority in the practical field of plainsong, Dame Laurentia was
consulted by scholars the world over, from cardinals to seminarians,
from Cathedral Masters of Music to youthful missionaries in the
African jungle. French and German abbots and abbesses rub
shoulders in the monastic chronicle with priests from America
and nuns from Dublin, and nicest of all, perhaps, the correspondent who applied for further enlightenment to the author of
The Grammar of Plainsong:

'To the Superior Benedictine Monks of Stanbrook.
    'Very Revd. Sir, will you kindly explain what DJ and P
mean, and 5, 4, 3, 2, 1 which appear in a Grammar of Plainsong? Believe me, Revd. Father, your obedient servant,
Egbert Roberts, Principal Bass, Italian Church, Hatton
Gardens—31 years. Please give your blessing.'

It was to the choirmaster of Solesmes, Dom André Mocquereau,
a musician of outstanding ability and reputation, that Dame
Laurentia always turned for advice and guidance. As a schoolgirl,
during a brief visit to Solesmes, she had fallen under the spell of
Gregorian Chant. Her early letters to Dom Mocquereau usually
consist of a large sheet of paper divided vertically, the left-hand
column containing her queries written in French, the right-hand

left blank. His replies take the form of oracular exclamations in Latin, French or English, penned in what she styled 'his most neumatic handwriting'. On a single sheet one meets with 'Oui. Bon—You are right! Yes! Parfait. Oui, oui! Bene!'

Throughout her life, Dame Laurentia retained a sense of the liveliest gratitude to Dom Mocquereau and considered his principles unassailable. But she was no blind enthusiast. In September 1904 he paid her a visit from the Isle of Wight, where the Solesmes community was in exile. One afternoon he outlined his idea of introducing into future plainsong editions his own supplementary rhythmic signs. She listened intently. After a long pause, her cool grey eyes met his intense black ones as she finally asked in warning tones, 'Vous vous rendez compte, mon père, que cela va créer beaucoup d'ennui?'

The quick reply came with the force of a pistol-shot, 'Je le sais. J'ai tout prévu. Je continue.' The storm she had foreseen broke in the following year.

One other musical influence in the person of the German Father Henry Bewerunge, Professor of Ecclesiastical Music at St Patrick's Seminary, Maynooth, was to enter her life in September 1902. For twenty years he spent Christmastide at the monastery, giving lessons to the 'organ-grinders' and directing much of the musical activity of the house. His influence upon Dame Laurentia was possibly even greater than that of Dom Mocquereau. Their letters record the stages by which they reached 'perfect agreement' on the debated subject of rhythm. 'We used to quarrel violently in the early years!' she remarked later. 'Plainsong may be the most peace-giving music on earth, but there is nothing like its theory for putting people on the war-path.' He finally admitted somewhat grudgingly that there was precious little difference between Dom Mocquereau's theory and his own, and as proof thereof translated and published, with Schwann of Cologne, Dame Laurentia's *Grammar of Plainsong* in which so much prominence is given to Dom Mocquereau's rhythmical principles.

Two further incidents should be mentioned; the first tells of her friendship with other contemporary plainsong scholars in this country, the second speaks for itself. On 12 February 1897 the eminent expert, Dr G. H. Palmer—'the best scholar of the subject

26

in England', as Dame Laurentia described him—came to Stanbrook for the first time.

'Mr Worth and his friend Mr Palmer (Anglican clergyman) left here today delighted with their visit,' reads the entry in the chronicle. 'The latter is a great musician and admirer of Gregorian Chant. He had just copied out of the Sarum Missal two lovely responsories and had them in his pocket; he showed them to Dame Laurentia who was delighted with them especially as we had none for the next two Sundays—our books having been sent to the binder. They were at once copied and learnt. They are *Igitur perfecti sunt* in Dom. Septuag. and *Volens Noe* in Dom. Sexag.—both so pretty.'

No wonder the visit was recorded by the chronicler. The effect on those expected to transcribe and learn at such short notice two lengthy responsories must have been electrifying.

Thirty years later Dame Laurentia spoke of her outside work for the Chant to Sydney Cockerell:

'I have some new pupils—the choir of Besford Court, a wonderful college for mentally deficient boys. I was asked to take on sixteen for regular lessons, but it was impracticable, so I arranged to have two very nice masters once a week, and the boys once a month. They come the thirteen miles on a motor-lorry and enjoy the trip. Poor boys, they are very pathetic, but wonderfully under control. The mentally deficient seem to be musical! Yesterday I had a choir of thirty-one men from Banbury, and next week-end my dear mill-hands (nineteen of them) are coming from Lancashire. They have been saving up their shillings for months.'

Tongue in cheek, he offered to extend her classes, 'If you are so good to the mentally deficient, I think I must send you a weekly contingent from Cambridge. They will include some of the cleverest men in the University. Perhaps you could give them a course in plain speech.'

With her readiness to help whensoever and whomsoever she could she combined a strange power of conveying friendliness even towards people whose acquaintance she had not made in person. She was immensely pleased at the news of the projected biography of her old friend Edmund Bishop; and when a year before her death his biographer, Nigel Abercrombie, wrote to ask her if she could contribute any material, she at once set to work. Few who saw her or received letters from her in her last years could realize how handicapped she was by age and illness; her courage and gaiety hid her sufferings, and the letters she despatched to Nigel Abercrombie in her beautiful cursive writing gave no hint that the hands which wrote them were rigid with arthritis and that the writer herself was unable to move an inch without aid. It was Edmund Bishop's eager disciple of half a century before who promised to help:

'I had a lively correspondence with E.B. beginning about 1905 and possess a number of valuable and characteristic letters. . . . I must be only one of many whom he inspired with his advice and real assistance. I found that one way, at any rate, of securing his interest was to make a fairly intelligent mistake on an historical point. That fetched him.

'The letters are again in my hands, rescued from the archives, and I shall be glad to send them to you, after looking through them. They will require care in editing, for we got on gossipy terms and his views on men and things were not all suitable for publication!'

Their correspondence had arisen out of the work dearest to Dame Laurentia's heart, the publication and editing of the Worcester Antiphoner, known affectionately as 'Wig'.[1] This thirteenth-century manuscript, the only complete English Benedictine Antiphoner in existence, was of especial interest to her because it came from Worcester where, if anywhere, the pre-Conquest English tradition of the Office and the Chant may have been preserved. It was Dom Aidan Gasquet who had advised her to submit her work to Bishop. Both by precept and example the latter taught Dame Laurentia to write. He demanded of her discipline, an untiring quest of historical truth, perseverance in

[1] From its official title, *Antiphonale Monasticum Wigorniense* (MS F160 in Worcester Cathedral Library).

the face of obstacles, independence of judgement, and a sense of personal responsibility for every assertion made. The footnotes to Volume XII of the *Paléographie Musicale*, where the Antiphoner and its Introduction were published during the years 1922 to 1925, bear witness to his pupil's aptitude.

There is a Lewis Carroll quality about Edmund Bishop which comes out strongly in his correspondence with Dame Laurentia over the Worcester book. No printed page can convey any idea of his even, shapely, yet difficult handwriting in which the tiny letters grow larger and larger under the influence of his excitement until a word or two will start out from the page six times as large as any that precede, only to be followed by a microscopic word underlined three or four times which calls for a magnifying-glass. His use of italics, his parentheses, his jabberwocky, his playful humour, the delightful human compassion of the man, his whimsical oddities, his prejudices are all an essential part of 'E.B.'. They are left unaltered in the quotations which follow.

An innocent remark of Dame Laurentia's in a letter of 1905 first set the ball rolling. 'One wants now to get at the history of the English Monastic Breviary,' she wrote. 'I suppose we cannot get back further than the tenth-century revival.' It was a short letter. The reply came on eight pages of solemn quarto paper. In a learned dissertation, he established the fact that there was no such thing as a breviary in Dame Laurentia's sense of the word in the tenth century and concluded:

'The fact is we are in general downright ignorance as to the liturgical history of the Benedictines in England during this period . . . but I can't see why we need always remain so. *Est modus in rebus*: which I sometimes like to render: there is a right way of going to work in such matters (but it's commonly a long one, and the road is indirect). . . . But the point I must insist on is this: that this period of the history of the "Office" of the English Benedictines is really an uncultivated field.'

There and then he drew up for her a formidable plan of study. The Worcester book was to be a mere starting point. She must examine in addition no fewer than ten monastic Ordinals or Customaries of which he appends a list. Above all she should procure photographs of as many complete manuscripts as possible.

'Study carefully the original documents *first* and try to see what one makes of them oneself on paper; and *then* go to modern authoritative writers.' He cautioned her against the opposite procedure. 'What have I not had to suffer, in weary pilgrimages back to where I was before, by listening to "authoritative writers" and correcting myself by them. Don't mistake me: I don't say don't read 'em, don't use 'em, one *must, it's a dereliction of duty not to do so: BUT* don't think that just by reading 'em and then going to the documents just to furbish up one's pages with correct references, one has come to *knowledge.* No: "try the spirits", examine, verify, *try* 'em . . . and one not so infrequently finds one has to "try" them by a *renewed* careful study of the original documents oneself. Amen.'

When in 1914 Dame Laurentia was at last able to submit a first draft of the Introduction to the Worcester Antiphoner, he warned her:

'In these matters I am utterly unscrupulous—and have no regard for anything anybody may say or feel, as "mere" feelings: and on the other hand, I am utterly *callous* to any treatment I may get in the way of sharp, short, and pitiless *rejection* of "poor me", *and all* my words and works in this matter, my "doubts and queries", "notes and observations" and all the rest of it. Now let us begin by a preparation of mind:—utter callosity!'

His 'utter callosity' was soon in evidence. 'It is not to the purpose of this Preface,' she wrote in her opening lines, 'to enquire into the Liturgy of the early British Church. It may be fairly conjectured that a Celtic rite prevailed borrowed from the Irish, with whom the British had constant intercourse.' Alas for the unfortunate word 'conjectured'! The doughty champion of 'Facts to correct Fancies' burst into the arena at full tilt.

'I should say: *omit* "It may be fairly conjectured"—You see one always indulges (I "always" indulge) in these send-offs—efforts to get under weigh (or "way"). And then I proceed, when the thing is done, to use the pen freely for cancelment.

'Besides "I" should say: What do we, you, I, anybody know about "*a Celtic rite*"? I believe the thing is all nonsense and the invention of such imposing ignorantines as Dr E. W. and Co. to whom our Catholic writers say humbly *ditto*. Eheu! When we don't know, don't let us seem to know: and above all, beware of the "dull (and pompous) *deceivers*".'

E.B. Item precor et obtestor. 20.v.14.

'What *joy* these letters have given me,' was Nigel Abercrombie's response to the correspondence. 'He rides his hobby horses—almost all of them; but he lets you hear notes of kindliness and simplicity and real godliness that were not so often audible in *the letters people have kept*. Especially I love his WISH in the Christmas letter of 1907 (Dec. 18)—"a thankful heart". He had it you know, at the very very last, and took it away with him out of this world; did they tell you? it is worth knowing.'

Dame Laurentia seemed able to liberate at once the personality of her correspondent, and their letters, in which each poured forth reminiscence and appreciation of E.B.'s inimitable self, might have been exchanged between lifelong friends. She did not live to see the publication of the work[1] but Bishop's biographer received her wholehearted encouragement in advance:

'Your letter delighted me,' she wrote immediately in answer, 'for it proved that E.B. was fortunate in his biographer. You cannot have known him, but you have the grasp of that unique personality. I had not realized that his letters to me were so revealing, but I see there the simple, *humble*, sincere man. In spite of his "rages" one recognized a deep spirituality—real godliness. You must have found that he had violent and often unreasonable prejudices, due mostly to his intense Englishness, and the smugness of Anglo-Catholic "scholars" in particular and of foreigners, v.g. Duchesne, brought on earthquakes and

[1] N. J. Abercrombie: *Life and Work of Edmund Bishop* was published by Longmans in 1959.

tidal waves of fury. "They don't know and they don't know they don't know," was an expression I remember.'

It was not only those who asked for help who received it; she sensed the need for guidance even in those who least expected to find it. The writer Peter Anson, for fourteen years a Caldey monk and ever afterwards torn between the pull of the sea and his love for the monastic life, called merely, he thought, to see her about the publication of one of his many books. 'This afternoon Abbess Laurentia invited me to have tea in the big parlour,' he wrote. 'This amazing old lady sat behind a grille and entertained me with wise, witty and shrewd conversation. It was an experience I shall never forget. *What* a personality! I don't think I had ever realized how unique she is. She smoothed out—with no apparent effort—several little matters which were troubling me. I realized I had given her my confidence without knowing it.'

From the circumstances of her life, indeed, it would seem that God called her to an apostolate rare in the life of an enclosed nun, an apostolate which often lay outside the bounds of the visible Church. Whether her contacts were with members of the household of the faith or not was of small consequence to her. In the chapter of his Rule on the reception of guests, St Benedict bids his disciples show special attention to poor men and pilgrims, 'because in them is Christ more truly welcomed'. From the earliest ages of Christendom monasteries have been the refuge of the poor, and in spite of the efforts of the modern welfare state the needy continue to knock daily at the door for food and drink. But there is a poverty—and never was it more rife than in these days—far more deplorable and pitiable than mere material destitution. People come to a monastery nowadays largely unaware of their hunger for that 'supersubstantial bread' of which St Matthew speaks. They hardly know why they come or what it is they want, but rarely are they sent empty away. The contacts Dame Laurentia made with the world were never of her own seeking. There is a hint of weariness in a petition to be excused from increasing the circle of her acquaintances. 'I think it would be wise for me to live up to the illustrious people I already know before adding to the list. So don't send me anyone else at present,' she begs in one of her letters. Nor did she ever try to disguise the fact that her friendship, her advice, her correspondence were all animated by a spirit essentially apostolic. She would be all things to all men in order to gain all men for Christ. To Sydney Cockerell who held religious views widely divergent from her own, she once sent a photograph of her brother James:

'The photograph is of my priest-brother, the most angelic person I have ever known. To him I owe my vocation or rather the possibility of carrying it out, for he was a great power in the family and persuaded my father to give his consent. You will probably think that no merit, but to me it has meant everything.

'Talking of vocations brings me back to our correspondence. I suppose the real difference between us is one of values. To me the supernatural point of view is the *real* one and the one which concerns the best part of one's nature. Looked at from this point one's "use" and influence have a wider range than if one thinks only of the natural side of things. Of course in the days when I left the world I scarcely realized my own powers, but with growing experience I feel convinced that I have used them *much* better than I should in all probability have done in the world. But such thoughts have little or nothing to do with *vocation* and its subtle and almost irresistible force. After all it is "une affaire du cœur", if you like to call it so, for one's heart cannot rest in earthly things if the call is heard. We do cut ourselves off from lots of beautiful things, but only to get nearer to Him who made them. And the compensations for the natural joys of life are wonderful and exactly corresponding. It is no ordinary privilege to be the mother of a soul. I cannot say more today, and to no one else would I say so much.'

In view of all that has been said of Dame Laurentia's wide interests and all-embracing sympathies, it is scarcely surprising that four of the longest and greatest friendships of her life were with non-Catholics—Ivor Atkins, Canon Wilson, Sydney Cockerell and George Bernard Shaw: all four had made their appearance in the monastic precinct before the end of 1907. Of Ivor Atkins who remained her devoted friend for over fifty years, there are few written records. He was a very near neighbour and for many years, especially during the chaplaincy of that excellent musician Dom Gregory Ould, he visited Stanbrook almost every Saturday; there was therefore little need of correspondence to maintain a friendship constantly kept in such good repair.

It was over music that Atkins turned to her in the early years, to enquire about the pronunciation of Latin in sacred music or, as he resurrected di Lasso for the Worcester Musical Festival of 1914, the source of the composer's liturgical text. Dame Laurentia's labours in transcribing the plainsong melodies sung at Worcester Cathedral in mediaeval times were immediately put to advantage; in 1916 he wrote asking her to copy one out, 'I want to do it on Thursday next and to teach it to the boys as early as may be. Last Thursday we did the Wig form of *Jesu, nostra redemptio.* . . . It is very different from Sarum and as usual very much better.' In return, copies of his own compositions and of his edition of Bach's *Little Organ Book* came her way.

If anything, their friendship became closer after Canon Wilson's retirement as Cathedral Librarian. In 1926 they decided once again to clothe the Great 'O' Antiphons (sung at the end of Advent) with the melodies that had resounded in the Cathedral four hundred years earlier. 'I wrote and told Canon Wilson,' Atkins informed Dame Laurentia on 17 December, 'that you and I had worked together at the 'O's as a memorial to Mrs Wilson. . . . I sent him, too, our schemes and the printed words of the 'O's.' When Worcester Cathedral Choir visited Stanbrook in Advent 1983, they sang these very settings with great artistry.

Common interests led to common friendships. One day in 1928 Ivor Atkins brought a Dr Craster to meet Dame Laurentia. Friendship was struck up at once and within a fortnight Dr Craster was sending notes from the Bodleian Library that were invaluable for her current work on the Barking Abbey Ordinal. Her interest in mediaeval studies and all 'Wigorniensia' continued unabated to the end of her life. Early in 1942 she wrote excitedly to Sydney Cockerell, 'Have you seen that the oldest copy of the Rule of St Benedict extant—eleventh century—written in England, is now shown to have belonged to Worcester Cathedral? It is now Hatton 48. Sir Ivor Atkins came over in great elation . . . to tell me.'

Atkins' longstanding association with Stanbrook was one that not even Dame Laurentia's death could sever. In his courtly way he asked permission in August 1953 to continue to call as of old, and forthwith arranged with an infectious, almost boyish enthusiasm to hold a discussion, not on music as one might naturally expect, but on St Augustine's interpretation of the psalms—a proposal hardly surprising from such a fine Christian. When he died shortly afterwards, a great link with the past was broken, and the Stanbrook community lost a true friend.

It was he who first introduced to Dame Laurentia James Wilson, Canon of Worcester Cathedral, as she relates in a letter to Sydney Cockerell, dated 14 April 1931, when recalling the occasion of their first meeting:

'My old Canon apparently still lingers. Yes, we first met in that year of great grace, 1907. I have just looked up my record of letters and visitors for that year, and find that it was on April 15. . . . Sir Ivor Atkins sprang on me a large party—the Canon and Mrs Wilson, a Mr and Mrs Archdeacon of ——, Mr Sayle, and at the end of the meeting three enormous Wilson "children" were brought in by their mother,— Margaret, Hugh and Steuart! After that the old man came regularly and I got to know him and his well. Mrs Wilson was a great soul, worthy of him, and an ideal helpmate. This has been one of the enriching friendships of my life, and I feel that most, if not all of the gain has been on my side. I wonder why so many wonderful gates have been opened for me, and why two of the very greatest gifts should have been given me in one year. No one can say, but I am humbly thankful.'

She made the acquaintance of this 'fine and delightful old man, one of the sincerest and humblest people I have ever seen,' when Canon Wilson at the venerable age of seventy-two became Librarian of Worcester Cathedral. He proved a frequent visitor at Stanbrook, and a large packet of letters survives to bear witness to the constant interchange between them. At once he had set to work to restore and classify some six thousand old manuscripts stored away in boxes in the Edgar Tower, and he made some remarkable discoveries among the pieces of vellum used to reinforce old bindings. Each fresh find was brought to Stanbrook in triumph and it was Dame Laurentia who identified what has become one of the most valuable treasures of the Cathedral Library, an eighth-century fragment of an anthology of St Gregory the Great's writings compiled by his contemporary, Paterius. Manuscripts of Paterius have never been common and until she identified the Worcester fragment none was known to exist earlier than the Ghent manuscript of the late ninth or early tenth century. Historically Worcester's Paterius manuscript, *De Expositione Novi et Veteris Testamenti*, is of the utmost importance as witnessing to the great popularity of Gregorian writings in the English see to which Alfred the Great was to send the autograph presentation copy of his translation of Gregory's *Cura Pastoralis*.

Dame Laurentia's work on the Worcester Antiphoner was naturally of great interest to Canon Wilson. Her study of the rubrics led to discoveries of early architectural details of the Cathedral. She pointed out, for instance, to Canon Wilson that the instruction for the Palm Sunday procession clearly implied that the triforium was open to the nave, and that there had been a large porch over the north door in which the cantors, four or five monks and boys, had stood to sing the *Gloria laus*. Upon examination, though all traces of the porch had been destroyed by the rebuilding of the wall, there were revealed the Norman nook-shafts of a wide north door.

Beginning with mediaeval fragments, dust-covered rolls and accounts, their friendship grew ever deeper. 'My father admired her beyond anyone else except (perhaps) my mother,' wrote Steuart Wilson. 'They were divided by so narrow and yet so impassable a cleft of creed, and united by an interest and a Christianity that was greater than anything.' She entered into Canon Wilson's interests, scholarly, human and divine, with all the generosity and zest of her cordial nature. In their biography of Canon Wilson, his two sons have reproduced a charming anecdote related by Dame Laurentia, touching in its simplicity and expressive of the understanding sympathy which bound the two friends. 'One day, I think in 1919, he came over unexpectedly, and I took down whatever we were interested in at the time,' she wrote, 'but he put it aside saying: "I haven't come about books today; I have come for consolation," and then, weeping like a child, he told me that Mrs Wilson had just gone into a home for a serious operation.'

The confidence he put in her in respect to his human relationships extended to the deeper things of the human soul. It is obvious from his letters (her replies after 1916 have unfortunately perished) that as the years went by, their deliberations passed from the problems of time to those of eternity, and finally to the theme expressed in the words of the psalmist: *Cogitavi dies antiquos et annos aeternos in mente habui*—'I thought upon the days of old, and I had in my mind the eternal years,' as the Vulgate text runs. The immemorial years of life everlasting had long possessed Canon Wilson's mind, and in his last days his thoughts dwelt continually on what theologians call *in termino*. He was acutely conscious of his being in progress, in a state of evolution, of hearing a perpetual 'forward' in his ears, and he hesitated before the agonising problem of the great riddle of Death. On his eightieth birthday Dame Laurentia sent him a quotation from Isaiah xliii, 2, in her own beautiful script: *Cum transieris per aquas tecum ero, et flumina non operient te*—'When thou shalt pass through the waters, I will be with thee, and the rivers shall not cover thee.' These words became the constant theme of his meditations.

He opened his mind freely to her regarding the difficulties his faith experienced in throwing the bridges over into an unknown future. On August 27, 1927, he wrote to her of the death of an old friend whose funeral he had just attended:

'It was a strange experience: we had met and talked a little only a few days ago, and now she, or her earthly body, lies in Steep Churchyard: and mine will lie there, next to hers, very shortly. What a mystery the future is! I am as certain as I can be of anything that my spiritual life goes on; the product of such infinite ages of past evolution; but in what form it is not given man to know. Christ did not reveal that, and science is still dumb. We can but trust in God. He has guarded and guided me for ninety years, and I am content to leave myself in His merciful hands.

'Farewell, dear friend. Remember that my experience is

very very different from yours. Death is the one experience that we shall have in common.'

It was not to be farewell for another three years, however, and in the following year he again reverted to the text of Isaiah which had been her gift to him so many years before, pouring forth in his simple, beautiful way the doubts that assailed his mind, as they assail most human minds at the contemplation of eternity. A famous saint of modern times, the Carmelite Teresa of Lisieux, has related how thought of the future beyond the grave plunged her for years in the blackest darkness, a source of conflict and torture of which the only outcome appeared to be total annihilation. Her one response was a dry, courageous, almost despairing *Credo* which is the very essence of hope. In his measure, it was in that same cry that Canon Wilson found refuge:

April 22, 1928

'My very dear friend,

'You sent me on Nov. 6, 1916, a beautifully written card. *Cum transieris per aquas tecurm ero, et flumina non operient te.* It stands, and has always stood, on the mantelpiece of my bedroom, and is the last thing I look at every night. I shall not forget you. I always think with special thankfulness, of your friendship for me, and of your prayers for me. I am not so weak as your letter shews that you think I am. I can still write a legible letter, though it is a long process; and I feel inclined on this Sunday morning to write to you.

'This Easter tide has brought me much quiet happiness. I am, as you say, in "my time of waiting": I cannot tell when I shall be called, but it must now be soon. And your quotation from St Cyprian fits in with one of my moods, and enriches and sanctifies it. I have *two* moods. In one of them I see, or seem to see, the invisible world of Spirit as the only reality. I see this life as a mere episode, full of some unknown meaning in eternity. I resign myself to that thought. I know, or think I know, for certain that I shall soon be in another spiritual world, in an eternity which is quite other than infinitely prolonged time, and is quite inconceivable by our present faculties—a kingdom of God which will solve all our problems. And I am quite content. I had no notion, not the faintest, of life before I was born, and I have no notion of the life after death until I die. But Christ lives, and whatever in me is truly Christ-like must live in some way. I am content with that.

'But this is not my only mood. I am unable to conceive of life as apart from some sort of matter. I cannot think of last year's daffodils, or last year's butterflies, or the dear dogs that I loved (and still love) when a boy, as still alive. And men stand in an unbroken line with these. How can I picture anyone as a spirit? To think of it is to think of some attenuated form of *matter* or ether. We lose ourselves. This is a real difficulty.'

He had not yet spoken his last word on the subject. At Christmas, 1930, Dame Laurentia sent him a little lavender bag, made with her own fingers and filled with lavender from the Stanbrook enclosure. Newman once playfully likened scent to the angels in so far as, unlike music, it is communicated to the apprehension in a single moment of time. Certainly nothing can be more evocative, and it filled her old friend with delight. Taking up his pen, this grand old man of nearly ninety-five wrote a letter of final valediction:

STEEP, PETERSFIELD
Dec. 28, 1930

'Dear Dame Laurentia,

'When Louisa, my attendant, came into my bedroom on Friday she exclaimed, "Lavender, someone has sent you lavender!" It has scented my room ever since. And your letter radiates peace and happiness in the same way. I send all my Christmas cards, when I have thoroughly enjoyed them, to Sister Margaret for her patients and children, in the Solomon Islands. I think I shall send your bag of lavender too.

'I have been alone this Christmas: all my children and grandchildren (but one) being away, Grace at Cannes, Steuart in the U.S.A. and so on. But I am not feeling alone: reminded of so many absent friends by letters etc. Your card, now for some twenty years, adorns my chimney piece in my bedroom and always reminds me of you.

'Do you know some lines of Whittier that I met with?

> *Death is but the covered way*
> *That leadeth unto light.*

I think that a happier image than "crossing" a river. A covered way, dark, unknown, must be travelled by every one, and travelled alone: and at the other end *Light*.

Very truly yours,
James M. Wilson'

On 15 April 1931, he passed *ex urrbris et imaginibus in veritatem*—'out of shadows and reflections into truth'—into that mode of knowing and being about which, to use his own phrase, he had been so 'inquisitive'. It was the twenty-fourth anniversary of their first meeting in the parlour at Stanbrook. Canon Wilson died in the late forenoon. At 11.30 in the refectory at Stanbrook Abbey, by a strange coincidence, the voice of the reader was heard declaiming the passage of Scripture allotted to that day:

The Book of Isaiah, Chapter the Forty-Third

And now thus saith the Lord that created thee, O Jacob, and formed thee, O Israel:

Fear not, for I have redeemed thee, and called thee by thy name: Thou art mine.

When thou shalt pass through the waters, I will be with thee, and the rivers shall not cover thee.

2

The Nun and the Humanist

IVOR ATKINS, Canon James Wilson, Sydney Carlyle Cockerell and George Bernard Shaw could reckon their association with Dame Laurentia in terms of fifty, twenty-four, forty-six and twenty-six years respectively, friendships severed only by death. With the first two, the Master of Music and the Librarian of Worcester Cathedral Library, this confabulation of friends flowed along in serene harmony; with the tempestuous Creative Evolutionist from John Bull's Other Island, the exchanges whether in sunshine or storm were exhilarating—he enthralled her with his genius and wit, enraged and distressed her with his misty mysticism. With S.C.C. however, the bearded scholarly infidel—the term he applied to himself and defined with characteristic exactitude as 'a man without any set creed'—the friendship was one of 'mutual benediction and recompense' kept in excellent repair by visits and regular correspondence from their first meeting on 5 January 1907 until 9 August 1953, a fortnight before her death. Although their differences were acute and frankly admitted, they never came into open conflict. The man whose enduring monument is the Fitzwilliam Museum, Cambridge, repeatedly assured her that he was little more than 'a mere camp-follower and despoiler of the slain, a skulker, loving ease', to which she returned a reassuring 'We will not quarrel about your attainments. I am quite satisfied with them.' Undeceived by such approval, he warned his biographer, Wilfrid Blunt, not to try to make a great man out of him after his death, because he wasn't. Whether a great man or not, his letters are first-rate, a happy mixture of the erudite and trivial, completely honest and completely natural, and from first to last written, however hurriedly, in a striking cursive script described by the eminent palaeographer E. A. Lowe as 'very legible and full of a curious, almost feline, grace, the performance of one well versed in the secrets of calligraphy'.

In 1954 S.C.C. made a gift to the Stanbrook community of the complete correspondence, bound in eight volumes.[1] For the first seventeen years of their acquaintance neither knew each was keeping the other's letters, but early in 1924 it was agreed that the survivor should inherit both sides of the correspondence, with perfect freedom to keep or destroy the chronicle of so many outward events in their two lives. The epithet 'outward' has been chosen with deliberation, for what strikes any reader who knew Dame Laurentia well is the strange combination of communication and reserve in her letters: she is diffusive of self and enclosed at the same time behind a barrier of reticence, very much in view, yet almost wholly concealed.

No greater contrast can be imagined than that between the citizen of the world and the nun who was to dismay him by the assurance that she knew not and cared not to know what lay on the other side of the Malvern Hills visible from her cell window. A man in his fortieth year, Sydney Cockerell's life had already been crowded with more interest, activity and enjoyment than could be met with in the lives of ten lesser men. Together with the business acumen that made him a successful partner, at first in his family's business from 1889 to 1892, and later with Sir Emery Walker as process-engraver from 1900 to 1904, he possessed artistic tastes, love of adventure and a compassion for mankind which won for him from Lady Burne-Jones the title of 'Friend of Man'. A fervent disciple of Ruskin both in art and life, companion and friend of William Morris, he had worked for five years among the poor of Southwark, acted as secretary to the Kelmscott Press from 1894 to 1898, and to Wilfrid Scawen Blunt during the two succeeding years. Not content with travelling in France with no lesser guide than Ruskin himself, and at various times touring France and Italy with William Morris, Emery Walker, Lady Burne-Jones, W. R. Lethaby or Bernard Shaw for company, he added shipwreck in the Gulf of Suez ('It was

[1] Selections from this correspondence have been published in *The Best of Friends: Further Letters to Sydney Carlyle Cockerell*, edited by Viola Meynell (Rupert Hart-Davis, 1956).

distinguished of you to be wrecked in the Red Sea,' Dame Laurentia commented. 'You must have wished for Moses and his rod.') and two sojourns in Egypt to the list of his experiences. From his close friendship with Morris he had derived that love and expert knowledge of mediaeval manuscripts which made him one of the greatest authorities on the subject. At the time of his meeting with Dame Laurentia he was acting, to use his own phrase, as Dyson Perrins's 'hired man', examining and cataloguing the valuable collection of mediaeval manuscripts in the latter's library at Malvern.

Both men, experts in the field, had heard that the thirteenth-century English Psalter belonging to Oscott College, Birmingham, was temporarily housed at Stanbrook, only five miles from Davenham, the home of Dyson Perrins, whose name was a household word as that of the head of Lea & Perrins, makers of the famous Worcester Sauce. On that wintry Eve of Epiphany, Dame Laurentia was sitting in her cell when the monastic silence was shattered: 'I remember hearing Mr Perrins's car snorting under my window and wondering who and what had come to disturb the peace.' There emerged two visitors, announced as Mr Perrins and Mr Cockerell, who asked if they might see the Oscott Psalter. Abbess Caecilia Heywood and Dame Laurentia received them, but had to explain apologetically that they had returned the manuscript, so were unable to do more than show photographs. 'That meeting was prepared *ab initio et ante saecula*, and our respective guardian angels (for though you have no patron saint, I rejoice to think you have a special Angel) must have been looking for the immediate occasion, and having chosen the Oscott Psalter must have moved it about until they got it to Stanbrook.'

So wrote Dame Laurentia as she looked back upon that momentous meeting. Momentous it was for the house in general, for Sydney Cockerell became one of the most generous benefactors in the practical direction of arts and crafts that it has ever known. At the time, Dame Laurentia knew nothing of his history or circle of friends—to her, he was simply a collector of ancient books and manuscripts. She was yet to learn that he had been present in the company of Browning, Christina Rossetti, Ford Madox Brown and W. M. Rossetti at the unveiling by Holman

Hunt of the Rossetti memorial in Cheyne Walk in 1887; and again while Ruskin and Browning removed their hats and stood bareheaded in each other's presence at an exhibition of the Old Watercolour Society in Pall Mall; he had journeyed to Yasnaya Polyana to talk with Tolstoy; he had met men and women from all over the world, but never an enclosed nun behind a double iron grille until that January day.

In spite of his later strictures, one suspects that S.C.C. was 'parshial' to the nun in the cage, as Daisy Ashford would put it. After all, its function was as practical and obvious as that of grilles in a post-office, bank, or cashier's desk, and should need no further justification. It made for freedom and convenience on both sides. A strictly contemplative house has the right to protect its own life. True, the grille was a challenge, a sign of contradiction— 'To what purpose is this waste?' Yet experience was there to prove that it frequently promoted rather than prevented confidence, and the nun behind the bars was often able to bring counsel and healing to many in sore need of both. In days of swift change it is well to beware of

> . . . superficial notions of evolution,
> Which becomes, in the popular mind, a means of disowning
> the past.

T. S. Eliot expresses a truth that is perennial: only within the last hundred years has Darwinian scientific theory been elevated to a popular philosophy of life which, in its turn, may be exploded. Let it suffice that S.C.C. admitted that the Stanbrook enclosure provided 'rather a nice cage' and the grille neither constricted nor intimidated him. He was quick to see that in fact it simplified human relationships: 'She seemed to know everything,' he wrote of his new friend, 'not only about her own special studies, but about all that was taking place in the world outside. Our meetings were as frequent as circumstances would allow. Sitting on either side of a double grille we discussed both grave and mirthful topics with mutual enjoyment.' From the outset he realized that he had met his match in liturgical scholarship; on the other hand, his expertise in mediaeval manuscripts and in printing outstripped hers. As a result, they struck a bargain:

'I believe you enjoy these investigations,' he wrote in April, 1907, 'and I warn you that I am going to take all the advantage I can of your readiness to place your learning at my disposal. In return I will joyfully give any help I can in matters that are more or less within my province. Let us take this position for granted and let there be no more thanks between us. I was quite embarrassed yesterday by the pretence that they were due to me rather than to you. Any book I have is yours to borrow, "*mihi et amicis*". I trust you implicitly not to put it in the hands of anyone who does not know how to turn over the leaves or that the paint and gilding must not be touched. Ladies of the world are terrible defaulters in these respects—and the monks (I say nothing of the nuns) of old days were little better —but at Stanbrook I think the right spirit prevails.'

She immediately accepted the terms of the agreement:

'Let me say, once for all, that you are welcome to any little help I can give you. I agree to the terms you propose regarding our position of mutual assistance, and I will never say thank you again, but you must allow me to have my own opinion as to who is likely to be the gainer by the compact. I shall take due advantage of your kind offer regarding your books, and shall consider it a point of honour to see that they are reverently handled.'

The many monographs and beautiful Roxburghe Club facsimiles, now treasured in the Stanbrook scriptorium, testify to the generosity of the various scholars who found their way to the Abbey as a result of that January day: Henry Yates Thompson brought his *Hours of Yolande of Flanders*; Michael Tomkinson of Kidderminster an exquisite thirteenth-century Bible, the smallest ever seen; Dyson Perrins the contents of his priceless collection of manuscripts in regular instalments. The nun behind bars met these citizens of the world on equal terms: after all, what to them was a mere academic exercise, to her was daily life, as she was soon to prove. S.C.C. brought for her inspection an illuminated Commentary on the Psalms neatly written in a good Italian hand of the twelfth century, author unknown. Going straight to the solid wall of the 217 volumes of Migne's *Patrologia Latina* in the library—still in constant use—she ploughed through the indices, followed every trail from Apostolic times until Pope Innocent III, and finally ran her prey to earth: Odo of Asti, disciple of St Bruno of Segni, bishop, monk and abbot of Monte Cassino (d. 1123), among whose liturgical works Odo's Commentary had mistakenly been included. Collating Migne's text with the manuscript, she discovered the printed matter incomplete. The full text in S.C.C.'s possession was otherwise unknown. Naturally her find greatly increased the value of his manuscript. Small wonder that he valued her opinion.

He kept her busy. Within six weeks of their meeting, he was submitting his work for her criticism before printing off the sheets, and at the same time sitting down to study her publications: her *Grammar of Plainsong* of 1905, translated into French, German and Italian, still a standard work reprinted as recently as 1962; *Gregorian Music*, a folio volume with facsimile illustrations of manuscripts, printed at Solesmes in 1897, a book long out of print but never superseded; and at least a list of possible subscribers for a book he was unable to afford—the *Antiphonale Monasticum Wigorniense* from the Worcester Cathedral Library, which she was editing at the time. On 17 February he asked Dame Laurentia to proof-read his editing of four leaves from a Dominican manuscript, the Beaupré Antiphoner—'a book that would make your mouth water. I know nothing else to compare with it'—and the Noyon Psalter. By return of post, she had fulfilled the task:

'Your descriptions of the MSS are excellent and so complete. I have noticed three slight printer's errors, but everything else is perfectly clear:
  p. 24 (the Dominican book) Vesper for Vespere
  p. 54 (Noyon book) footnote 3rd line aureas for aëreas
  p. 70 (Beaupré) No. 11 Missus et for est.
What a gorgeous book the Beaupré MS must be, so full of life and invention, to say nothing of the skilful execution. I cannot forgive Ruskin for taking the volume to pieces; it is a comfort to know that they have been restored as far as possible to their original form.

Do you think it likely that the illuminations of the Paduan Gradual were done by Benedetto Bordone, who is said to have adorned the great choirbooks of St Justina's? It is a pity there are so many lacunae in the Gradual, but all the text and music that remains is very interesting.'

To attack Ruskin, S.C.C.'s idol from youth, was a risk but he took it in good part: 'I am relieved to find that you have no more formidable errors to tax me with. Ruskin, whom I knew and revered, was unhappily a great Philistine where books were concerned, and other sins besides that of the breaking up of the Beaupré Antiphoner must be laid at his door. The Psalter and Hours of Isabelle of France were his also, and he gave nine leaves of it to Oxford & 3 to a friend in America. They have all now been restored to the volume after an infinitude of trouble. . . . Dear old Ruskin, what naughtiness he was capable of! and dear old Carlyle, how peevish and fretful! I love them all the more for it.'

The marginal pictures in the Beaupré book had disappeared: S.C.C. suggested that a disapproving abbess had possibly removed them, and added:

'I hope that the Lady Abbess and yourself would not be in favour of knocking off the grotesque heads and monsters from the interior walls of mediaeval churches (I say nothing of the exterior gargoyles). The drolleries in the service books were done in the same spirit and though they may seem out of place to modern ideas they were quite in keeping with the spirit of the middle ages and I do not think we have now any right to meddle with them; unless perhaps when they happen to be offensively indecent, which is of course sometimes the case— mere harmless frankness should I think be let alone.'

She at once repudiated the charge of vandalism:

'Lady Abbess would not for all the world deface a single grotesque head or monster or gargoyle: neither would I. I quite revere the dear little beasts in the Oscott book, but I wish the cock were not in the lower margin of "Cantate Domino". In the Worcester Processional (to be published in our facsimile) there is a charming page of refined and lighthearted humour.

47

In the genealogy according to St Luke, you will remember, every sentence begins with *Qui*, and the good old monk varies his Q's in the most surprising fashion. You must see it next time you come.'

While this interchange of liturgical scholarship was to continue throughout their lives, he more knowledgeable on the artistic, she on the textual aspects of mediaeval choir books, their erudite game of battledore and shuttlecock never ceased to be light-hearted. Of a Book of Hours, he asked: 'Can you identify Saint Ossanus? He is a young dandy who carries a thigh-bone, & wears the latest cut of Italian smart clothes and is very clean and well brushed about the hair. He should belong to Padua or Bologna or Ferrara c. 1480.'

Sydney Cockerell's community of goods did not stop short at Dame Laurentia; his invitation to share was extended to the whole house. As heir to the ideals of the Pre-Raphaelite Brotherhood, and disciple of the man who had established as a guiding principle that 'the highest wisdom and the highest treasure need not be costly or exclusive', it was to be expected that Sydney Cockerell should be attracted by the handicrafts traditionally associated with the monastic life. 'Forms of execution which are merely prettyish, and those which, pretending to mastery, are nothing better than slovenly and slapdash' he hated as much as Rossetti, and he set himself at once to inculcate the highest ideals of workmanship among the nuns. Within a few weeks of his first acquaintanceship with the house he was supervising, criticizing and giving all the help and direction his generous nature could devise, in printing, photographic reproduction, formal script and illumination.

'I believe I can enter as fully into the aspirations of your community as many who are not infidels,' he wrote banteringly, 'and I should like to be helpful in matters that are to some extent within my province, and especially in the revival of the spirit of craftsmanship which exists, but needs direction, at Stanbrook, and which I have found to be so painfully absent in other religious houses at home and abroad. Of course there are heaps of difficulties on account of your seclusion and the remoteness from proper teachers and from the stimulus of seeing actual things instead of merely pictures in books—but some of these difficulties we must try to overcome.'

He meant to be taken at his word and he was, being straightway bombarded with requests for help in technical printing processes. From this it was but a short step to introducing the printers of the community not merely to beautiful specimens of printing from the Kelmscott and Doves Press, but to famous printers, to St John Hornby, and above all, to 'the most distinguished master of the craft of printing, and the man of the most consummate taste in such matters'—Emery Walker. Under their direction, given freely and with the utmost generosity whenever it was needed, the printers learned, not merely how to print—they had been doing that ever since Father Laurence Shepherd set up the printing press in 1876—but how to design pages of type and produce books of fine workmanship. In addition to both these benefactors, Sydney Cockerell introduced Katharine Adams to give instruction in bookbinding, and familiarized the artists with the work of the best contemporary illuminators and scribes. But he could be formidable, as in his letter of May, 1907: 'Dame Domitilla must persevere, and so must the bookbinders and the rest. I feel strongly what I said—that whereas women like Miss Kingsford and Miss Adams whose lives are fretted with all sorts of distracting pleasures and duties, and who have besides to win their bread and butter, may be excused for occasional short-comings, the nuns of Stanbrook are bound by their position to do work without a flaw. Next time I shall perhaps bring a piece of embroidery to startle those who ply the needle and to raise their standard.' He then pushed his ideas a little further. 'I can do nothing myself with my hands (I consider one plays the organ with one's head, not with one's hands)', she had told him in the early days of their friendship, 'but I delight in all those artistic principles and ideals which after all apply to my music as much as to your art.' Thus encouraged, he asked: 'I suppose my scheme for fostering the arts at Stanbrook must not include dancing, though I consider it *a religious exercise* which would do you all no end of good?' Teresa of Avila had danced for sheer joy before her Lord in the Carmel of St Joseph's—but Teresa was a Spaniard, Laurentia a Scot. All the same she was to lend him Ellen Terry's

book on the Russian Ballet with this comment: 'Funny book for
a nun to lend you, some people but not you, would say! This
Russian dancing interests me enormously, in its close relation to
music. I like the ancients' division of the arts into two triads.
1. The beautiful realized in repose= architecture, sculpture &
painting. 2. Beauty realized in movement—music, poetry &
dancing. Simple of me to specify such categories to an art-student
like you! It seems a far cry from Russian Ballet to Plainsong,
but there is a parenté in the laws of rhythm.' Neither of them
could foresee the fruition of those ideas on 21 March 1981, the
close of the Benedictine Centenary year, when eleven of the
community gave a beautiful performance of ballet-cum-mime
in the atrium and Chapter House at Stanbrook, showing the Rule
of St Benedict as a Dance round the Torah, its epigraph drawn
from St Gregory Nazianzen, 'Dance the dance of David before
the Ark of the Covenant, for I believe that such a dance holds the
mystery of walking in the sight of God.' For once, Sydney
Cockerell would have added a heartfelt, Amen, Amen.

It cannot be denied that he was a forthright critic. The man
who told Thomas Hardy he ought to stop waxing his moustache,
met an unknown lawyer with a frontal attack on legal jargon
('Testamentary dispositions': what *terrible* words! Why can't you
say 'will'?), and corrected the letter of a young Stanbrook nun, a
total stranger, with the abrupt question: 'Why "grateful"
thanks? If they are not grateful, they are not thanks. Why two
words when one suffices?'—such a man acquired a not-undeserved
reputation as being a rather redoubtable opponent. Perhaps least
of all did his friends escape. As Siegfried Sassoon said of him, his
devoted friendships were 'tender yet astringent, brusque but
adoring', and to be contradicted by Cockerell was an education.
It was well that Dame Laurentia positively welcomed honest
criticism: years later, when elected Abbess, her nuns paid her the
highest compliment any religious superior could receive: 'You
could say to her face,' they said, 'what you would not dare to say
behind her back.' Sydney Cockerell did not hesitate to say it, and
said it within weeks of their first meeting. She had presented him
with a copy of her *Saint Egwin and his Abbey of Evesham*, published in 1904 under the critical direction of Edmund Bishop.
Although the style is naturally of its period, the study retains its

validity as historical and liturgical source-material—the Bibliography shows that she consulted every known MS except Bodleian Digby 112. It would seem that she inscribed S.C.C.'s copy: 'To Sydney C. Cockerell Esq. with the compliments of the author.' She was unprepared for his downright: 'I am not at all pleased with the unsisterly inscription. I think you might have left out Esq!' And three days later: 'If that was meant to be a very nice inscription, I must ask for an unfriendly one if you ever give me another book—to see whether I shall like it better. I never know what "compliments" mean. Is it that one is complimented on the addition to one's library?'

On 1 August 1907, he confessed that his interest in arts and crafts was temporarily on the wane: 'I am for the moment rather absorbed in another matter, having suddenly arranged to marry Miss Kingsford. I put all the proper arguments before her, and quoted what you had said about the awful time my wife was likely to have, but she persisted in accepting me.'

Dame Laurentia's immediate felicitations made piquant allusion to the legend of the martyrdom of St Ursula and her eleven thousand companions in a letter sure to be appreciated by one who had often enjoyed the elaborations to which the story lent itself in mediaeval illuminations:

'I simply can't tell you how pleased I am with this morning's news, for I did not like the idea of your going through life alone. 11,000 friends are all very well, but they can't make a home! Let me then congratulate you most heartily and wish you and Miss Kingsford every blessing and happiness. I should like also to congratulate her and to say that, in spite of my nasty remark which you repeated to her, I am quite sure she will be very happy. I wonder if this is the answer to one's prayers for you. I hope so. That you have made an excellent choice I have no doubt, for Miss Kingsford is so thoroughly in sympathy with all your tastes. I almost feel as if I knew her already, having heard so much about her and seen so much of her exquisite work, but of course you will bring her to see us some day. . . . With kindest regards and renewed congratulations on your engagement (though it does put a stop to your being a Monk!).'

No sooner was the engagement announced than Kate needs must call on Dame Laurentia—'I am calling her by her second name,' S.C.C. explained, 'as my brother Douglas has married a Florence.' Scared of being 'a fool and a discreditable frump' as she put it, Kate's fright vanished from the first moment of their meeting. 'How lucky it is that this is what always happens,' she afterwards said, 'in the presence of a really human being.' For her part Dame Laurentia found her guest 'not a bit shy or silent, and we got on excellently. I like your Kate *very* much, and so does Lady Abbess,' she reported. 'I told her she must come to see us with you sometimes, that is, if we are ever to see you again.'

Their wedding at the little mediaeval church in Iffley, Oxford, was fixed for 2 November. 'I am so glad you have chosen that lovely old church, but I am terribly disappointed in you about the date of your marriage,' Dame Laurentia wrote on 4 October. 'How could you, a student of kalendars, consent to All Souls' Day? It is altogether weird to me. The best part of the world (including Stanbrook of course) will be singing dirges and requiems round catafalques, such as you see in your MSS, and ringing knells. But I suppose it can't be helped as Kate has settled it, and "Ce que femme veut, Dieu veut!" At Iffley, at any rate, you will have the echo of old Catholic prayers hanging about you, which will fit in with the other Catholic prayers that will be offered for you.' In face of this objection, the pair yielded and moved the date to 4 November, the festival of SS Amantius and Modesta: 'I am afraid their appropriateness begins and ends with their names, though these are almost miraculously suitable,' Dame Laurentia at once wrote. 'St Amantius was Bishop of Rodez in the 5th century; St Modesta was Abbess of St Symphorian's, Trèves, in the 6th century.'

To this, the bridegroom lugubriously replied: 'I fear they never met, but no doubt they were always thinking of each other.' He cheered up however when Dame Laurentia reminded him that 4 November was also the feast of a modern St Charles: 'I have seen the shrine of St Charles Borromeo at Milan,' S.C.C. wrote, 'but I didn't know that November 4th was his date—not quite inappropriate as he was Carlo and I am called Carlie in the family—short for my second name Carlyle, which my father gave me for love of your fine old dyspeptic fellow-countryman.'

Before the wedding, the bridegroom had to put in fifteen statutory days of residence in Iffley, which he did very pleasantly: 'Dinner on Sunday with the dons of Brasenose, a nice set of fellows. Tea yesterday with Horace Hart at the University Press. To Maidenhead today to see my friend Dunn, a great collector of manuscripts, and the purchaser of the Crosby Hall document I coveted with the signature of Sir Thomas More. Lunch tomorrow with Gilbert Murray, whose translations you have read. . . . On Saturday I go to tea with Mrs Furneaux, the daughter of Joseph Severn, to see relics of Keats. The parson is rather civil. He came and invited me to supper again on Sunday, but I was engaged. Otherwise we might have come to blows over some little matters in his morning sermon, which I went in to hear.' George Dunn had shown him an exciting recent acquisition: a thirteenth-century manuscript of Reading Abbey. It was only a week before S.C.C.'s marriage, yet not only did he sit down there and then, make copious memoranda, send them with queries—why the importance of James and Maria Salome at Reading?—but was bold enough to write and ask the owner if he would lend the actual manuscript to Stanbrook. This he did on the spot. Certainly S.C.C. had a way with him. 'I love books that have *all sorts* of things in them as this one seems to have,' Dame Laurentia wrote in acknowledgement. 'Reading Abbey was dedicated to St James the Great, hence the prominence given to him and to St John and to their mother Mary Salome. I notice among the days for extra good things the Transfiguration, which was, I thought, a delicate attention of the monks towards their Patron.' Mention of the 'extra good things' reminded the writer of the approaching wedding-feast and led to this inventory of Reading luxuries:

'What can *brachinelli* be? (I must ask someone after the wedding-breakfast!) I suppose there was no obligation to partake of each of the 7 fercula. Fladones, flatones, or flaones i.e. *flawns*, I always imagine to be a species of pancake; at any rate they were made of flour, eggs, milk and butter. *Corneus* sounds as if it got its name from its shape—perhaps cream-horns! *Losenges* must have been the mediaeval equivalent to Fuller's creams! *Russoles*, the glossaries say, were "dainties called by that name", which leaves something to one's imagination, but they were some kind of pastry thing, for there is an entry in the Abingdon accounts of flour to be delivered to the cook for making them. It is sad when the list begins to come down to white beans and then to beer.'

George Dunn solved *brachinelli*, as being barley cakes seasoned with Cholsey malt. Whether malted barley cakes figured on the menu of the wedding-breakfast is left unrecorded. It was left to Katharine Adams to send an account of the 'quiet doings on the 4th'—which is all that S.C.C. said of the day. He and Kate were far too engrossed in a honeymoon that ended only with the end of the year. Naturally marriage altered the pattern of S.C.C.'s life and his relationship with others. There is a subtle shift of emphasis in Dame Laurentia's Christmas letter of 1907: henceforward first Kate, and in due course the three Cockerell children, would figure frequently in the interchange of news:

'While I have a quiet half-hour let me send you my very best greetings for this your first married Xmas, and in greeting you I of course greet Mrs Cockerell too. You know that my wishes for you are not empty things. If I might put into words my prayer for you, this is the Xmas gift I should like to give you: the full and perfect faith in Him without whom we should not have known the graces and joys of Xmas. This is the best thing I, or anyone, could wish you:

Gift better than Himself God doth not know,
Gift better than his God no man can see.

You may think my wish is quite unlikely ever to be realized, but I may be allowed to hope.'

The opening of S.C.C.'s world on to ever-widening horizons was further emphasized when, in June 1908, he was appointed Director of the Fitzwilliam Museum, Cambridge. For the next thirty years he lived in Cambridge. 'A scrounger of genius' as someone called him, he succeeded in creating one of the finest museums in existence: 'I found it a pigstye; I turned it into a palace.'

Connoisseur of fine arts as he was, S.C.C. was an even more expert connoisseur of people. He was not the man to neglect valued friends however busily he might collect new ones, and his letters to Dame Laurentia suggest that with her his friendship reached a deeper level than with almost any one else. He had always wanted to share his interests and enthusiasms, especially his admirations for certain people, but this was not so simple as it sounds. Unlike him, she was no avid collector either of books or friends. Early in 1907 he had sent her a catalogue of his doings: seven and a half hours in the House of Commons seated next to the Australian Premier to listen to the Irish debate; next day to Boni's lecture at the Royal Institution on the Forum with marvellous slides taken from a balloon; one night with St John Hornby to talk about Chartres; next night with Frampton the sculptor; breakfast with Wilfrid Blunt followed by an entrancing ballet at the Empire; a walk in Richmond Park—heard the cuckoo and saw herons nesting and red and fallow deer. Did she envy or pity him, he wondered? Her sole reaction was a laconic: 'I neither envy nor pity you. What a whirl you live in! I wonder how long people can last at that rate? When do you get time to *think*?' It was a good question. She could be liberal and broad in outlook and sympathy—as Bernard Shaw said of her, she was an enclosed nun without an enclosed mind—but no claim of friendship, no literary charm or intellectual excellence could deflect her from the one aim she strove with conscientious and simpleminded purpose to fulfil: a life of holiness. Possibly it was just because her life was hidden with Christ in God that it acted as a magnet to draw the world she had abandoned, but once she had decided that any person or thing might interfere with her high ideal, she could be firm to the point of intransigence.

Greatest perhaps of all S.C.C.'s enthusiasms was his veneration and admiration for Leo Tolstoy. In a letter of 12 April 1907, only three months after his first meeting with Dame Laurentia, he asked: 'I wonder what you think of Tolstoy of whom I am so great an admirer that I travelled all the way to central Russia in order to be in his company for half a day! If I do not forget I will show you a copy of a letter written to him by the late Grand Mufti of Egypt.' Without waiting for a reply, on the spur of the moment he slipped into a parcel of printing specimens a few stories by

Tolstoy 'that could not fail to win approval' as he afterwards apologetically explained.

Her acknowledgement was more than a trifle disconcerting: 'If I had answered the letter in which you asked me about Tolstoy,' she wrote, 'I should have told you frankly that his works are not at all on the lines in which my reading lies, though I have no doubt there is a great deal that is excellent in them. However I know what you have sent me is all right, for I can and do trust you implicitly not to put before me anything that would be inconsistent in the least degree with the principles upon which our life is based and which you grasp and appreciate so fully.'

Her closing remark was no empty flattery, as is shown by the answer she received in which Sydney Cockerell rose to the defence of his hero:

'Tolstoy is a man who has lived with the principle *Homo sum humanum nihil a me alienum puto*—and he has now after immense struggles and wrestlings arrived at that serenity of mind and indifference to worldly annoyance that comes only to the very wise and the very simple and the very religious, and not always even to these. One has only to meet him to feel that he lives on a different plane from most of his fellows—a plane in which love of family and love of country are entirely merged in love of man and love of God—though what God is, or whether there be one God or more than one, he told me he did not know. If you would ever care to see some notes I made —dull enough—after my visit I will send them to you.

'Of course I should not ever send you anything that I could suppose to be inconsistent with your course of life, but your phrase "inconsistent in the least degree with the principles on which our life is based' may mean more than I should wish it to mean, and if so you must keep me within bounds. Strictly interpreted it might cut you off from I know not how many things that I should consider uplifting and widening to the soul whether of a nun or of an unstable inquirer like myself—from Homer, from Plato, from Chaucer, from Wordsworth, from your own Sir Thomas More's *Utopia* and from Ruskin whom you told me that you read. But I hope that the principles that you refer to are not so narrow as this and that you count all those upon your side that are on the side of the angels, whether wittingly or not.'

In a rather lame response, 'You need not fear,' she assured him, 'that our principles will be too narrow; they admit all the people you mention and, generally, all that is elevating. All you say about Tolstoy is very interesting, and some day I should like to see your notes. It is a marvel to me how so wise and good a man should be in doubt about the Unity of God. But it would take too long today to say a lot of things that occur to one's mind in this connection.'

Self-confessedly she found it difficult to appreciate religious difficulties, and argument or apologetic she heartily disliked. To human eyes, her life seen as a whole, was possibly all too easy. She never knew deprivation or heavy affliction. An adored youngest child, she left home at the age of eighteen—'the most desolate day of my life'—and passed from one closed circle to another, from a deeply loving Catholic family to a monastic community where her gifts of mind and heart very soon secured her a position of unchallenged eminence and authority. At Stanbrook she was trained in a well-constructed theology and in a deep but uncomplicated liturgical approach to God through contemplative prayer. She never had to face the fundamental problems that beset even those brought up in the Christian faith, and consequently she had never formulated let alone answered many of the tremendous questions that life poses. This betrayed itself naturally enough in her monastic life. Her lack of experience, her ignorance of what is today called 'the human situation' led at times to an incomprehension, an inability to appreciate and meet with compassion those undergoing really searing trials on their way to God. Possibly her schooling was at fault—it is odd that she had no true insight into poetry, and one wonders what she made of Hopkins's 'terrible sonnets':

> Selfyeast of spirit a dull dough sours. I see
> The lost are like this, and their scourge to be
> As I am mine, their sweating selves; but worse.

Protected and privileged as she had always been, she found it difficult to project herself into the mind of another who, in deep sincerity, was following a path divergent from her own. After the hierarchical, social and religious upheaval of the last thirty years, it is no virtue in us to see the necessity of respecting even diametrically opposite positions. The marvel is that with her Victorian upbringing and environment, Dame Laurentia was, in many ways, so ahead of her times. In 1914 when she rose to the office of Subprioress, S.C.C. had written: 'I prefer you as Sister Laurentia, and until you are elected the first Lady Cardinal and have lovely scarlet apparel I shall not be impressed by any promotion—always excepting that of Abbess of Cambridge.' Yet when she was elected Abbess of a mere Stanbrook, he confessed that he felt a little afraid of her new dignity and grandeur, even though he knew she would remain her old self. She would hate him to call her by any new title, she told him, and she invited him to her Blessing according to the Metz Pontifical, adding: 'The change is going to make no difference. The dignity is in the office, and I have a proper respect for it even in myself, but Heaven forbid that I should ever stand on it with anyone, least of all with my friends.' She never did, and yet all unwittingly she tended to throw into the shade and underestimate the talents of younger recruits who, in her own field, had the advantage over her of a rigorous mental discipline and training. There were those who wondered whether, after a lifetime of affection, trust and appreciation, she could stand up to comfortless days sure to come. They did come. In the diminishments and ever-increasing incapacity of old age, she showed her growth in holiness and her true mettle. Not in vain was her patron Saint Laurence, the man who jested as he was roasted on a gridiron: she gave no place to self-pity, ignored her physical condition, and with magnificent courage kept her finger on the pulse of the community, infused her own spirit of joyful serenity, and governed the house in peace to the day of her death.

As she had never known human agony and spiritual turmoil, her summary dismissal of the Tolstoy stories sent by S.C.C. is the more easily understood, but her reaction was purely personal and many Benedictines—certainly in today's post-Conciliar atmosphere—would heartily disagree with her findings. Dom Bede Griffiths, for instance, the well-known author of *The Golden*

String, has expressed views on the suitability of Tolstoy as
monastic reading which support those of Sydney Cockerell. After
discussing the novels of Jane Austen, the Brontës and George
Eliot as providing not only desirable relaxation and the corrobora-
tion of personal spiritual experience, but also 'a continually
renewed discovery of the way the eternal laws of the spiritual life
work themselves out at different times', Dom Bede Griffiths
concludes: 'If we want to find the novel in the full extent of its
greatness, we have to go outside England and turn to Russian
novelists. . . . Their psychology is of a depth and complexity which
no English novelist can approach. But above all, the religious
motive is set free.' He singles out for special praise Tolstoy's *War
and Peace* and Dostoievsky's *The Brothers Karamazov*. 'Tolstoy
and Dostoievsky were both men seeking God and their novels
are the record of their search. Dostoievsky went furthest and in
The Brothers Karamazov he presents us with a world which has
found its centre in Christ. Tolstoy never found peace and died in
a last frantic effort to escape from a world in which he could no
longer believe. But this makes the search for God all the more
moving. . . .'

What would Dame Laurentia have said to that? She might
have reconsidered her standpoint; or again, she might not. Anyone who knows how discreetly and carefully she selected her
reading throughout life cannot feel certain that she would have
followed Dom Bede's reasoning even for herself, much less
assented to it in practice where the rest of the community were
concerned.

S.C.C. had always shared with her his books and ideas: but
above all else, he now wanted to share his living friends. 'Some I
have to keep apart,' he wrote, 'others I wish to bring together.
There are several I should very much like you to meet, but they
are mostly poor and you are too far from where they live.' Had
his wish been fulfilled in one instance, the story might never
have had its tragic ending. Writing to Dame Laurentia from
Cambridge on 15 April 1928, after the death of Charlotte Mew,
he said: 'Assuredly you were nearer akin than any two of my
women friends, being both possessed of that essential virtue
Charity, together with the gift of understanding, to a very rare
degree. I am very sorry that you never met—I believe you would

have been fast friends at once. She longed to join your faith but could not bring herself to accept its dogmas. When she stayed with us here she sallied forth to the R.C. church.'

Charlotte Mew, described by John Masefield in 1923 as 'the most distinguished of the living women writers', the author of two slender volumes of poetry of deep beauty, lived in great poverty with her sister Anne, 'exquisite and dauntless spirit' to quote Charlotte's own phrase, in a manner which Sydney Cockerell aptly compared with the life of Charlotte and Anne Brontë. As Dame Laurentia and Charlotte Mew were never able to meet, he adopted the next best expedient and occasionally allowed each to see the other's letters. In 1919, having invited Charlotte Mew to stay at Cambridge, he expressed anxiety about Dame Laurentia's health, adding that he had urged her to go out into the world again for the good of her soul and body in much the same way as the wicked go into retreat in religious houses—'but I am afraid,' he added, 'that I shall never break what to me (though not to her) are her prison bars.'

Charlotte Mew's letters in reply show an extraordinary appreciation of the freedom that the so-called prison bars really represented:

'As to Cambridge, Dear and very kind Mr Cockerell, I am not going to Cambridge . . . or to any other strange houses, or to see any other strange people, for the good of my soul or body, any more than your Sub-Prioress, for the good of hers, is going back into the world,—which perhaps both of us know well enough.

'"In schort" as Mary Stuart would say we are "au contrarie", but with good and trusty reasons behind us. WE ARE FIRM—and happy enough, if you could only believe it, behind our "prison bars". I am really sorry to hear she is not well (and the poor infidel cannot pray for her recovery!).'

A few years later S.C.C. again sent her two letters of Dame Laurentia's with the remark: 'I defy you to discover for me a nicer, more understanding and more saintly lady.' Unlike him, she did not stop short at the person who wrote the letters. Her swift poetic intuition pierced beneath the surface and reached from the particular to the universal. She saw the contemplative life for what it is—the power of Moses praying with uplifted hands on the mount to save from destruction the people of God fighting in the plain: 'I hasten to return and to thank you for the privilege of reading the precious letters. Do not "defy" me to find a more wonderful lady—I shall not try; but as for saints, this same lady would agree that the grey cloisters here and there hide—how many? to whom perhaps we owe it that this wicked old Earth is not yet in ashes.'

Within a year of her sister Anne's death, Charlotte, worn out with ill-health, poverty and tragic cares, in a moment of deep depression put an end to her own life in March 1928. Feelings of charity and tenderness filled Dame Laurentia's heart and over-flowed into her letters when she heard of the tragedy: 'Poor Charlotte Mew. What a sad end to a brave struggle, but if life has taught me one lesson, it is that of judging gently—and in spite of appearances. I read your tribute in *The Times* and liked it. Those verses *Exspecto resurrectionem* were my favourites in her book:

> 'Oh! King who hast the key
>   Of that dark room,
> The last which prisons us but held not Thee,
>   Thou know'st its gloom.
> Dost Thou a little love this one
>   Shut in to-night,
> Young and so piteously alone,
>   Cold—out of sight?
> Thou know'st how hard and bare
> The pillow of that new-made narrow bed,
>   Then leave not there
>   So dear a head!'

'I am sure we were sisters in many of our sympathies. This will urge me to make a return by praying for her. I have been reading the poems again and they make me weep with their poignant note. How she must have suffered.'

Charlotte Mew had risen to the defence of her spiritual kins-woman behind the 'prison-bars'. It must be admitted that from the moment of his introduction to Dame Laurentia in the Stanbrook parlour, S.C.C. found no attraction in the idea of imprisonment conveyed to his mind by the grille, and the subject formed a topic of pleasing debate between them at intervals all their lives. . . . 'What a fraud you are,' he teased, 'to talk of cinematographs as though they were part of your daily existence! It is like your vivid description of Evesham which no one will believe you never saw. I begin to suspect that when Lady Abbess is asleep you fly over the hills on a broomstick, and inspect the wicked world that you have rejected.' 'It never occurred to me,' she replied, 'to think that I had not seen a cinematograph. I know exactly what it must be like, without having recourse to nocturnal broomstick rides. Lady Abbess thinks you rather limit my time for inspecting the wicked world, by confining me to the times when she is asleep; our nights are short. And do you think all her waking hours are spent in the endeavour to keep me off my broomstick?' Her opponent was too honest to deny that he had been struck at his first encounter with Abbess Caecilia and herself by their obvious happiness, and after some weeks asked if he might put a few questions about her life. This led to a series of letters, more revealing than any she otherwise wrote, which form an admirable vindication of the life of any contemplative nun:

'You need not hesitate to ask any questions,' she replied on 1 April 1907; 'if I can, I shall be delighted to answer them. You are quite right in believing that we are intensely happy. For my own part I believe no one on earth should be so happy as a nun. I even think we have quite the best of everything even in this world, for we get the hundredfold promised in the Gospel, in return for the little we give up, and our monastic life is a world in itself, full of wonders of its own, full of reality, and full of interest. Of course all such happiness presupposes a call to the life.'

If his aim had been to lead her to write an apologia for the choice she had made, he could not have set about his task with more unerring psychological insight. He gently informed her that he felt sorry for her. 'When I saw Stonehenge yesterday, and the hares playing on the downs (nine at one time) and the plovers and the larks overhead I was sorry that you were cut off from the thrill it all gave me.' An amusing skirmish ensued. Dame Laurentia's deep joy and irrepressible humour combine with her high seriousness and devotion to her monastic life to make her letters a rare and grand defence if one were needed:

'I could not help smiling at your regrets on Stonehenge,' she writes. 'You do not think of us, I hope, as caged birds (or lions); we do not answer a bit to that description. The only place where there is any impression of cutting off is the parlour, and we look on the grate as a barrier, not to keep us in but to keep you out. We are not debarred either from enjoying nature, though we have not the variety that you so-called free people can procure. Inside the walls of our own Paradise we have a lovely little bit of God's world, and enough living creatures to satisfy even St Francis. Hares are scarce, but we have delightful rabbits; and as to birds, our larks and nightingales are unequalled, and the thrushes sing here as they sing nowhere else, not even in Scotland, so that I pay them the compliment of calling them mavises. I say nothing of the beauty of the country itself, especially at this time. Besides these human and natural joys, there are as you suspect, others, better far. It might be difficult for you to understand the intense and ever-growing joy that a monk or nun finds in the Choir—*domus Dei et porta caeli*. You won't be sorry for me again, will you?'

A few days later came his answering riposte:

'I believe all you tell me about the joys and compensations of the life you have chosen. None the less, I *do* regard you as caged birds. You may tell me that we are all caged in some way, by fashion, by prejudices, by duties, by principles, by lack of health, strength, understanding, means etc and that you are free from some of the bars that enclose other women. Of course I admit it. And as to keeping *me* out I accept the situation cheerily and if you like you may say that it is I that am imprisoned on the wide earth. Until I know you better I shall still be sorry that you cannot see Stonehenge and the barrows of the ancient chieftains of that countryside, that you cannot see the British Museum, the National Gallery and Chartres Cathedral. . . . May I not be sorry that you miss these things?'

He had committed a blunder which she hastened to rectify. Memories of a journey to Chartres and Solesmes made as a young girl in the company of Dom Laurence Shepherd came flooding back. In her answering letter she corrected his false impression and ended by asking one of the most tremendous philosophical questions of all time:

'If you persist in being sorry for me, I suppose I can only hope that time will bring you to a better way of thinking. But in the meantime please take Chartres off the list of things to be sorry about, for I am happy enough to have seen that most wonderful and glorious Cathedral—one of the most delightful experiences of my life. You are right of course in saying that all men and women are more or less caged; the question is— what kind of people are the most free or the least caged? The answer will depend on what we understand by freedom.'

The questions he then put to her, probing deeply and delicately into the motives that led her to embrace the monastic state have, in large measure, provided the Preface to this book. A very pertinent question of hers however calls for more extended treatment. After referring to the indefinable mystery of 'vocation' and the obligation it entailed of praying for the world, she concluded: 'I wonder how much you believe in prayer?' That was a bold question to ask of 'the infidel'. In order to avoid any dissimulation he had plainly stated his religious position from the first. The correspondence in which each sifted and tested the other's beliefs is marked throughout by courtesy, sincerity and complete absence of rancour, but if the story of Dame Laurentia's activity has so far been one of almost uniform success, the story now to be told is one of seeming failure, failure in what to her was dearer far than mediaeval music, history or illuminations. She failed to christianize him.

If, moreover, in preference to all the other topics which might have been selected from their correspondence, that of their religious differences has been chosen, it is because the subject is one of perennial freshness, and because Sydney Cockerell raised questions which are engrossing many minds today. His attitude towards Christianity in the twentieth century curiously resembles that of many pagans in the second century; his objections likewise were all raised in the second century and all met and refuted by St Justin Martyr and Clement of Alexandria. It is interesting to see the problem restated in our own times.

'I am a man,' he had told her on 10 April 1907, 'without any set creed—too much in sympathy with all great religions to adhere exclusively to one, too much aware of the great mysteries to accept any solution of them. I have been to Assisi, as I told you, for love of St Francis and of the things he loved— and have looked at Damascus with more reverence for the sake of St Paul and his thirteenth chapter of First Corinthians. But I should look with similar feelings on places associated with Buddha and Confucius, and having seen a little of Mahommedans and known the late Grand Mufti of Egypt, who was one of the wisest, gentlest and most venerable of men, I am opposed to their being converted into Christians or into anything else but more enlightened Mahommedans.

'I tell you all this that you may realize what manner of infidel you are dealing with. . . .'

This plain statement is the expression of one who finds his ideal in the perfect man of antiquity—that combination of scholar, saint and gentleman—which, as Belloc has observed, can still exercise great power over generous minds, and especially such as are lovers of beauty. Why regard Christianity, it asks, as transcending the lofty moral teaching of Confucius, the profound wisdom of Buddha, the spirit of religion of Islam? Why enforce dogma? Why not allow that the different religious systems of the world are simply indigenous to climate, temperament, race or country?

To this she replied:

'It is very nice of you to tell me your religious views so frankly. You won't mind me saying that I think a man without a set creed is very much to be pitied. Whilst acknowledging all the good there is in the different ways which men have of expressing their religion, one cannot see how all can be equally right, —especially if we grant (as perhaps you do not grant) that God has made a definite revelation to men. I am not going to believe that you are a plain infidel, but I do not see where God and Christianity come in in your system. While St Paul and St Francis, and even the Buddhists and the Mahommedans have a very definite religious object in their belief and worship, are you less well off? And what about hereafter? Of course we do not believe in indiscriminate proselytizing, but I do believe that St Francis, after he had converted *you*, would have gone off to Egypt to try and make a Christian of your late friend the Grand Mufti!'

The letter is a delicate reminder of historical fact. When St Francis of Assisi stood before the Sultan and the Muftis at Damietta and fixed his eyes fearlessly upon their weapons and tools of torture, he did not speak of peaceful co-existence, nor did he crave any favour from their court. On the contrary he summarily demanded that all present forthwith renounce Mahomet. Sheykh Mahommed Abdu, Grand Mufti of Egypt, charming friend of Sydney Cockerell, would have fared in the twentieth century, so her letter insinuates, exactly as his ancestors had done in the thirteenth. But this her correspondent was not prepared to concede, and his reply shows him, in G. K. Chesterton's phrase, 'armed to the teeth and buttoned up to the chin with the great agnostic Orthodoxy, perhaps the most placid and perfect of all the orthodoxies of men', uttering the repeated cry: I do not know.

'My quarrel is not with Christianity but with the interpretation put upon it by the Churches—I can form no conception of the All-spirit, and any groping towards a conception leads me to something very different from the jealous God of the Hebrews. The worst of believing in any one religion is that it leads one to regard all other religions as wrong; I prefer to think that there is an element of truth, larger or smaller, in them all, and that the divine inspiration came not only to Christ but to

Buddha and countless others, that it comes indeed nowadays, as of old, to good men and women all the world over. As to hereafter I know nothing, nor whether I have lived before, and this ignorance does not worry me at all. Whether St Francis would have converted me I don't know. In the Grand Mufti he would have found a kindred spirit, and if there be a heaven for the just, they have merrily met there—they and Sir Thomas More and Joan of Arc and the Venerable Bede and Saladin and Galileo and many another.'

This attractive reply, with its all too easy simplifications, on the one hand rightly upholds what the Church has never denied, namely that in all times and in all places there has always been a certain true knowledge of God; and on the other hand altogether ignores the consideration that non-Christian religions are not so much false as incomplete, and must die before they can find their fulfilment in the Christian revelation; for Christianity is not a mere belief or philosophy but a life. In confronting Dame Laurentia with the religious experience of mankind divorced from biblical revelation, S.C.C. challenged her with the burning question of our pluralist society today: how interpret the fact that mystic experience of the highest order undeniably exists outside Christianity? How integrate it in a theological vision of the world and of God's plan for humanity? S.C.C.'s continual concern for the business of everyday living left him little time for profound thought, as Dame Laurentia had been quick to point out. His father Sydney John Cockerell, two months before his death in 1877 at the age of thirty-five, had written 'One feels so near to the great mysteries that surround our lives. . . . I resent with something like nausea any attempt on the part of well-meaning friends to reduce them to the level of my understanding —"to put the Almighty into a pint pot" as I think Kingsley very expressively if vulgarly says. What harmony there is between the best parts of all religions, and how much that teacher loses whose knowledge is drawn only from one sacred book—the Bible.' Clearly S.C.C. had made his father's philosophy his own.

In essence this is a refusal to allow that Christianity, an essentially historical religion, can be absolutely true or speak definitively about God the Supreme Being. It denies God's

sovereign freedom to intervene in the evolution of the cosmos
and in the drama of world history, to break the shackles of the
law of necessity that seems to govern the world, and reveal itself
in Christ as Love. It will not concede that all religions and
cultures ceaselessly advance towards the Incarnation and have
ever done so, so that from the Christian standpoint, all the spiritual
paths followed by human beings are integrated, fulfilled, taken
up and transfigured in Christ. And just as the Mosaic Law had
to be refashioned and transformed into the Gospel, so the
encounter between the cosmic covenant and the Christian faith
necessarily involves a passover, a passage, a death and a rebirth
to new life: this agonizing integration in which each appropri-
ates the truth of the other, must finally lead to enrichment and a
glorious resurrection. The unity which so many increasingly long
for will never be reached on the solid level of the intellect, for
the paradox of the Christian religion is precisely this: that love
appears at the very point where cosmic law and divine freedom
meet. During the last half-century, the Christian Church has
made significant efforts to meet the challenge. One has only to
read Thomas Merton's *Asian Journal*, and recall his intention to
visit Calcutta, Hong Kong, Dharamsala (to confer with the
Dalai Lama), Burma, Nepal and Japan to confer with Asian
monks—a plan cut short by his untimely death at Bangkok in
1968. In 1947, after twenty years spent in his monastery of
Kergonan, a French Benedictine went to India where he lived
as a sannyasi for the next twenty-six years; and in 1955 Dom
Bede Griffiths of Prinknash founded the Kurismulala Ashram in
Kerala, S. India. In the climate of the second Vatican Council,
no justification is called for, but it was perhaps fitting that S.C.C.
should raise the issue with a Benedictine nun, for it may well be
through the monastic orders that human society and culture will
pass into the Pleroma of Christ. Yet it was precisely this statement
that S.C.C. called into question. In a strange and intellectually
paralyzing argument *ad hominem* he suggests that the specifically
Christian virtues have been found and achieved without Christ.
His *integer vitae, scelerisque purus* has no need to face terrible
and difficult doctrines such as sin, the devil, hell or Redemption,
has no need, in other words, of Christ the Saviour.

Early in July 1907 at Sydney Cockerell's request, Emery

Walker had paid his first visit to Stanbrook. Dame Laurentia wrote to thank S.C.C. for his kind offices, whereupon the latter's unbounded love and admiration for the man who had been his business partner and ever remained one of his dearest friends, broke out into a question which under its apparent philosophical calm sounds a note of almost painful pleading not unmixed with reproach:

'Mr Walker is beaten gold, as Ruskin said to me of Morris. I have known him for twenty years, with constantly increasing admiration for his absolute genuineness and disinterestedness and real nobility of character. In his latter years Morris was never content to pass a day without seeing him. He is a Socialist, and as regards religion is as far from any harbour as I am. How do you account for it that so many of the best men one has known—men like Walker, Philip Webb and Morris himself—are in the ordinary sense *un*religious? *Ir*religious they are not, for they serve Stern Duty and various unknown and undefinable Powers that make for good. Are these men damned according to your Creed? Are you forbidden to believe that they are not only not damned, but specially sanctified—as it were tools that the Great Artificer delights to use for the bettering of the World?'

When her reply came it was, naturally enough, reassuring. What is truly astonishing, however, is to find a man with such an intimate knowledge of mediaeval literature and illumination —that fine flowering of Catholic spirituality—and possessed of an intellect of such high order, in total ignorance of the most elementary doctrines of the Catholic faith.

'Mr Walker struck me as being all you say,' she wrote, 'and I can understand your regard for him. What is the secret of his and your unreligiousness? To me it is a sad puzzle. Of course I do not know your religious history, but it seems to me that if you had been born Catholics your minds would have been in their natural atmosphere and would have developed on Catholic lines (I wonder if you are ready to slay me for suggesting such a possibility), but being, instead, thrown into contact with a form of religion which is largely negative, and being above it, you drift away into *un*belief or *dis*belief. Thank God, our Creed is wide enough to take in all men. We know that God's Light "enlighteneth every man that cometh into this world", and that each man is responsible for his correspondence with his own measure of light, neither more nor less, and each may be God's instrument. Not only this, but we believe that many men who seem emphatically outsiders, are spiritually members of the Church, through a sincere desire to serve God according to His will, and their own special light. Only, one would far rather have them altogether inside: "a blessing which I wish you all", as our Priests say at the end of sermons.'

Extra Ecclesiam nulla salus: no one can be saved outside the Apostolic Roman Church. That maxim first formulated by St Cyprian (A.D. 200–258) has been quoted in derision, pain or bewilderment by men who have never asked how the Church defined its own terms. It is simply a way of expressing the truth that the Church is the sacrament of salvation to all mankind, whether they are baptized or not. After discussing Jews and Moslems with their biblical roots, the document *Lumen Gentium* of Vatican II goes on: 'Those also can attain to everlasting salvation who through no fault of their own do not know the gospel of Christ or his Church, yet sincerely seek God and, moved by grace, strive by their deeds to do his will as it is known to them through the dictates of conscience.' The opening sentence of S.C.C.'s reply to Dame Laurentia's sober statement of Catholic teaching shows him only half-convinced, still fighting against the ingrained conviction that by the last verse of the Athanasian Creed—'This is the Catholic faith: which except every man believe faithfully and steadfastly, he cannot be saved'—the Church condemns teeming millions of good people to eternal perdition. Had S.C.C. been acquainted with early Church history, he would surely have realized that in formulating the doctrines of the Trinity and Incarnation for a church whose visible unity in faith and doctrine was accepted on all sides, the so-called Athanasian Creed directed its prefatory and concluding anathemas solely against those members of the Christian church who were deliberately contaminating the faith with their heterodox opinions. One can but admire the noble conscientiousness of the letter which acknowledged her explanation of the point at issue:

'I am very much interested in your reply to my question, which would seem to admit the possible salvation of unbelievers and of men of other faiths in spite of the last verse of the Athanasian creed.

'Those men I spoke of do indeed seem to me to belong to a Fides Catholica, wide enough to embrace all humanity and what is best in all religions—seeking only to do justly and to love mercy and to walk humbly in the presence of mysteries that they cannot fathom, and I should be grieved if you could not hail them as brothers treading much the same road as yourself.

'In thus questioning you—and many more questions may follow!—you will not suspect me of the smallest thought of attacking your belief. The fact that I know it to be as adamant, and unassailable, enables me to address you quite frankly and to seek out points of agreement. If it were not so I should be silent. Why should I be ready to slay you for suggesting that if my three friends had been born in your faith they would have remained in it? I feel myself some doubt about this, but I have no wish to slay you! Do you know that Morris and his companions at Oxford went very near to founding a monastery? It ended in their founding a shop instead—a more courageous thing in those days—and one that has had its influence all the Christian world over.'

During this first year of exploration, of testing and acceptance, agreement was reached on three points: chapter thirteen of St Paul's First Epistle to the Corinthians, St Francis of Assisi and St Thomas More. Yet nothing could emphasize their differences so forcibly as their agreements. It is Newman who, with that ironical subtlety of which he was a master, has pointed out with regard to the chapter of Corinthians, which represented the ideal of both Sydney Cockerell and Dame Laurentia, that St Paul 'discourses of that charity which is patient and meek, humble and single-minded, disinterested, contented and persevering. He tells us to prefer each the other before himself, to give way to each other, to abstain from rude words and evil speech, to avoid self-conceit, to be calm and grave, to be cheerful and happy, to observe peace with all men, truth and justice, courtesy and gentleness, all that is modest, amiable, virtuous and of good repute. Such is St Paul's exemplar of the Christian in his external relations; and the school seems to send out living copies of this typical excellence with greater success than the Church. At this day the "gentleman" is the creation, not of Christianity, but of civilization. But the reason is obvious. The world is content with setting right the surface of things; the Church aims at regenerating the very depths of the heart.' In other words, for the one, St Paul provided an ethical code of conduct, the mentally refined *beau idéal* of human society, for the other, the pattern of Christian perfection rooted in faith and love—and there is a world of difference between the two.

They both admired St Francis of Assisi. He loved the troubádour intoxicated with the natural beauty of creation, who marched singing through the world at the head of his army of friars, the Little Poor Man, one with the brotherhood of all men. She revered the hermit of Greccio and Mount Alvernia, the saint filled with nostalgia for God who saw the winged seraph descend from the heavens to imprint on his own body the wounds of his crucified Lord.

To both, also, St Thomas More, the cosmopolitan European with his wide human interests, eager intellect and energy, keen humour and scintillating wit was a force informing mind and conduct. Indeed, Erasmus' well-known description of More in his letter to Ulrich von Hutten opens with a passage which might equally apply to Sydney Cockerell: 'He seems born and made for friendship, and is a most faithful and enduring friend. He so delights in the company and conversation of those whom he likes and trusts, that in this he finds the principal charm of life.' The man who, as Director of the Fitzwilliam Museum, was to make his home the resort of men and women notable in almost every sphere of public life felt a natural attraction to the merry host of Chelsea at whose open table were to be found such men as Fisher, Grocyn, Lyly, Linacre or Reginald Pole; and especially did he love the father who was never so happy as when in the company of his beloved eldest daughter, Margaret. As a Christmas gift, S.C.C. once sent Dame Laurentia a reproduction of St Thomas's Meg: 'Dear and twice blessed Margaret Roper,' he exclaimed in an accompanying letter, 'do I not know her father's letters to her, including the one "wrote with a cole" almost by heart? "I never liked you better than when you kissed me last" etc. Roper's life of More has been one of my treasured books since I bought an old copy (1731) on March 7, 1891.'

Stanbrook nun that she was, Dame Laurentia likewise loved with a great and abiding affection the incomparable man on whose patrimony the monastery had been founded in 1623. Margaret in name herself, she too loved Meg's father, but above all, she loved the hero, prematurely aged and worn, who interrupted Audeley, his judge, in Westminster Hall, to win that supreme victory for England's Roman, Gregorian and Benedictine past, and the prerogatives of the See of Peter, which merited for him a traitor's death and crowned him with the Church's titles of Martyr and Saint: 'For,' he told the assembled Court, 'as St Paul said of the Corinthians, "I have regenerated you, my children in Christ", so might St Gregory, Pope of Rome, of whom, by St Augustine his messenger, we first received the Christian faith, of us English men truly say: "You are my children, because I have given to you everlasting salvation."'

While appreciating shared enthusiasms, neither of the two friends harboured any illusions as to the gulf that separated them: but whereas he remained the tenacious infidel, the pragmatist who measured truth by standards of social service, she longed to communicate the incommunicable gift of supernatural faith. One of her salient characteristics, surprising as it may seem in one so vigorous and alert, was moral patience. She knew how to wait. It was fifteen years before she again broached a subject that was never far from her mind. Only once during that period does the correspondence contain an oblique reference to the great wall of partition. In March 1910 S.C.C. was elected Fellow of Jesus College, and as such was allotted a stall in the choir of the ancient nunnery of St Radegund. 'I am afraid,' he wrote, 'that you will be rather jealous if not indignant, and that you will not think that matters are really mended when I tell you that my unbelieving nature will keep me from ever occupying my place in choir except when the chapel is empty or when my presence may be required for some special reason.' The playful irony of her retort makes no attempt to disguise how deeply she felt his lack of Christian faith:

'To think of you in a stall! I am thoroughly jealous, but not indignant, for I wish you a seat in a still better place if only you will make yourself fit to occupy it. You know how I regret your unbelievingness, but as it is the sad case, it is rather nice of you to save the stall and leave it to the ghost of its former occupant. I hope St Radegund will keep an eye on you. She will probably remark that you have a fair idea of how to be a nun, which might surprise her if she did not know of your friendship with Stanbrook.'

In October 1922 however, the concluding remark of a letter suggests that she deliberately sought to reopen religious discussion. She employed a delicate and rather amusing feminine stratagem, unusual for her. 'I was interrupted,' she writes cryptically, 'and in the interval I had a strange dream about you, though I rarely dream of my best friends. It was rather like St Monica's dream about St Augustine.' Her correspondent replied with the obvious and natural request:

'Do tell me more about your dream,' he urged. 'Did it promise that I should attain to religious conviction and felicity? With you for my guide? Under your guidance I would step further in that direction than with anyone else. But I am as little likely to be persuaded in your way as you are in mine—and the more so as most of the righteous men that I know and love and look up to are men of little faith, or of a faith that no Church could claim or define.'

Undaunted, she recorded her dream:

'My dream was this: We (you and I) were going, almost running, down a rather steep hill. There was a wall, or rather a Scottish dyke of slough stones, between us. Somehow I got the impression that you were becoming a most ardent *Christian*, and I rejoiced in that much. At the foot of the hill was a gate, and there we met without anything between us. I went up to you very eagerly and said: "But you have further to go. You have still to become a Catholic." You smiled (quite nicely!) and I awoke feeling happy about you. You must know that the fulfilment of that dream would be the realization of one of my dearest hopes. How gladly I would try to guide you in such a blessed path. It always hurts me to think that there is a whole side of your nature which is, shall I say, dormant? I don't mean that you have no spiritual side, for you have, but the absence of all reference to God and of all willing dependence on Him is such a want. The good men of little or no faith that you mention seem to me no argument. To me, they are what they are (admirable and lovable I know) *in spite* of their lack of faith—So now you know, and I leave the rest to God, doing my part by prayer.'

She must have found his response somewhat discouraging, and yet he could not, as he explained, be other than what he was. 'I find myself as sceptical and unyielding as ever,' he concluded, 'and if I change this attitude I think it will be because of waning powers and interests.' Neither was familiar with the other's language: terms needed defining. Her outlook and the words she used were entirely supernatural: when she spoke of faith she did not mean, as he assumed she did, merely a collection of doctrinal tenets to which the intellect and will either give or refuse assent. She hardly seemed to realize that the gifts she so easily spoke of, let alone their worth, were completely unknown to one who did not possess them. He realized it well enough, and candidly admitted the limitations of his vision:

'The spiritual values that to you are everything are largely beyond the range of my understanding when they do not, in some manifest way, lead to the bettering of the world. I do not deny, I very willingly admit, that this is due to defective apprehension, sympathy and vision on my part. But what one is one is, with all one's various limitations—and for the present at any rate I am shut off from entering into the feelings as well as the beliefs without which you would not be yourself but another being—I sorrowfully realize that this means that many a man and woman who has never seen you is capable of knowing you better than I do or perhaps ever can.'

One thing at any rate became obvious to both: the time was out of joint for further discussion.

She intensified her prayer while keeping up a regular and delightful correspondence concerning their manifold interests. In January 1924 the death of one of the community occasioned a letter which again gives a glimpse into her oft repeated petition for him. Dame Laurentia was Subprioress at the time, and as her letter relates, she slipped unobtrusively out of her stall in choir in order to assist a nun at the hour of her death:

'We have just lost our Dame Barbara Pattinson. She was a student at Newnham about 1881, and was a good classical scholar. She had a wonderfully tidy mind and was famous for arranging every moment of the day with great precision. She was just as precise in planning out the programme of her last days, and, strange to say, her plans came off. One of them was to have the *Alma Redemptoris Mater* and the Creed sung as she was dying. The last change came at a time when I was presiding in choir and I feared her desire would be frustrated. However, there was a free interval in which I ran up to the infirmary and sang her chosen pieces. She was unable to speak, but was quite conscious and so grateful. Half an hour later she was dead.—If I am taken before you, and can have my way, you may expect to hear me singing the Credo when your time comes, and you will have to join in.'

Her proposition evoked no answering consent, but by way of indirect reply, he enclosed in his next letter one from Henry E. Luxmoore, the well-known Eton master, 'a valiant spirit with very high ideals', in which the latter told the story of the vision of his parents seen by his youngest brother as he lay dying. In her acknowledgement of the letter, Dame Laurentia profited by the occasion to remark that the story confirmed belief in the immortality of the human soul, and bore witness to the truth that 'those who have gone before, cease not their love and care for those they have left'. Then almost brusquely, she assailed him with the direct question:

'Why do you and I never refer to the only things that separate us, that low stone dyke of my dream? For my part I abhor controversy, for which I have besides no aptitude, but I sometimes wish we understood each other's position better. I have a grudge against Ruskin for not having strengthened your faith, and I think his belief failed as his mental powers waned. To me it is all wrong for you of all people to have no supernatural faith, for you are so splendidly full of natural faith. Why is faith so difficult in divine things when it is so natural in human affairs? We *do* live by admiration, faith and love, and if we are blessedly told that the greatest perfection is love, we know that its foundation, in things human as well as divine, is faith. You must thank Mr Luxmoore for all this.'

Such a letter was a challenge and could not be ignored. Whether he wished or not, he was forced into a plain statement of his position, and this he proceeded to give:

'The story of his brother's death does not confirm anything, according to my stony judgement. This short and transitory life seems to me of such small account that I cannot imagine its being a basis for eternity, or for any continuance which would not be as remote from our terrestrial existence as that of a butterfly's from a caterpillar's. Now granted that a butterfly was once a caterpillar, if it does not remember being one, the relationship might just as well not exist. And as for the prospect held out, would not most people prefer *not* to meet again the friends and relations they have grown out of? Is it not generally very awkward to do this on this present earth? It is usually a failure and a mistake. Even the satisfactory reunion of lovers necessitates their going back to the age at which they parted, knocking the subsequent years of new loves and experience from one side, or adding some equivalent to the other. My imagination will not supply any working hypothesis, so I am content to remain among those who do not pretend to know. You invited me into this field of discussion, or I should have thought it was out of bounds, and indeed the dyke that separates us is one that cannot well be crossed by either of us. You take your creed on trust, asking only the authority and direction of the Church. That creed contains a series of tenets, which my reason refuses to accept. Of course I admit that there are countless mysteries beyond the reach of reason, but the resurrection of the flesh is not one of these and some of the other articles offer dogmas for which I can find no convincing foundation. And first of all God the Father, God the Son, and God the Holy Ghost, how are these "Persons" to be thought of? Do not the majority of the faithful conceive of them as magnified human beings, . . . with eyes, mouths, arms, legs and all the other attributes of male man? Is this not patently impossible? If it be impossible, why does not the Church declare it to be so? and what then becomes of all the beautiful literature of thrones, crowns and the rest, all the anthropomorphic visions on which we have been nourished? Once quit of all this questionable revelation, one is left with great overwhelming unexplained and inexplicable mysteries—the problem of limited space, the problem of unlimited space, the problem of our universe (let alone all the other universes) having been established out of nothing, the problem of the eternal past, that of an eternal future, or of a past or future not eternal— All these problems and very many others are (or seem to me to be) beyond the grasp of human understanding—and no religion (so far as I can see) makes them easier of solution.

'For people then of my sort of mind and imagination (both of course sadly limited), the only honest attitude is that of admitted ignorance, of admitted limitations, that cut us off from even the very beginnings of comprehension, where these stupendous mysteries, and the stupendous mysteries of life and death, are concerned—and to go about our business during our trivial existences as best we may until they end and we are forgotten, or are at most a name in a pedigree.

'And you must not think that I despise faith when I see it in others who really have it, and do not merely profess it, like blind sheep,—whether they be Christians, Mohammedans, Buddhists, Confucians or worshippers of Black Stones—A religion that we all now count vain raised the little city of

Athens to the topmost pinnacle of undying glory and gave Athens itself its name—as well as the Parthenon.'

Was her judgement at fault? To one who admitted that of Christian classics he had never even read St Augustine's *Confessions* 'beyond a glance or two', she sent a copy of that marvellous compendium of dogmatic, moral and spiritual theology called *The Penny Catechism* with the accompanying letter:

'Your letter interests me very much. It also consoles me somewhat, for though the points of difference between us are many and grave, you seem less of a heretic than I feared! As to the future life, surely one conceives of it as being on an entirely different plane from our existence here,—as an entirely new order of things, we being the same persons, but transformed, the body made spiritual and immortal ("glorified", as we call it) as Christ's Body was after the resurrection. As the conditions will be so different from those of our life here, I think we shall find no inconvenience in meeting even those whom we have outgrown. If I thought otherwise I should not want to go to Heaven.

'You surprise me by saying that the majority of believers think of the Three Persons of the Blessed Trinity as magnified human beings, with human members. If you look at pages six and twelve of the enclosed Catechism you will see what *the* Church teaches on that subject, and what every Catholic child learns as soon as it can read, if not sooner. The beautiful pictures of thrones and crowns and the descriptions of visions are symbols adapted to our understanding, and I am sure you are not the man to quarrel with symbols, nor with mysteries. We believe lots of things in the natural order that we cannot understand. No one knows what electricity is (except Lord Kelvin's famous pupil, and even he had forgotten!), yet we know something of its power, and use it in a thousand ways.

'We take our creed on the authority of the Church, but we are not asked to abdicate our reason; on the contrary we are required to study the motives of the credibility of the faith, and forbidden to settle down to ignorance. There are very few of the problems that vex the minds of men like you, in fact

79

there are probably none, that have not been faced and probably solved by the great minds of Christianity, such as St Augustine and St Thomas. I heard not long ago of a young man, not a Catholic, who had been through all philosophies, ending with Bergson, and who then coming on St Thomas found he filled up all the weak places in the other systems. But you would not read this kind of thing, so you will not give faith a chance.'

The reproach of her final phrase strikes a solemn note. *Facienti quod in se est, Deus non denegat auxilium*—God does not deny His aid to the man who does all that in him lies. In sending a Catechism, however, in the hope of preparing the ground for faith, she had been over-sanguine in her expectations, as the sequel proved. Gilbert Chesterton might provide a sight for men and angels as he wandered to and fro on the eve of his reception into the Catholic Church, his fingers stuffed into the tiny leaves of the mighty book, resting it on his forearm while he pondered it, head cocked to one side, but Sydney Cockerell?

'I was relieved,' he writes, 'to find you no more shocked by my unbeliefs than I was shocked by your beliefs! Of course we are both bound to be a *little* shocked and to wish it were otherwise —but there seems to be nothing to prevent our being as good friends as ever. I mustn't attempt any further discussion of our differences. There is no bridging the gulf between me and anyone who truly believes articles 69, 129, 134 and 100 (to take but four) in this official Catechism.'

The four offending articles are the Ascension of our Lord, the resurrection of the body, the existence of hell, and—needless to say—the infallibility of the Church.

In his autobiography G. K. Chesterton has related how, during his public controversy with Robert Blatchford, he found himself one night at dinner sitting next to 'one of those very refined and rather academic gentlemen from Cambridge who seemed to form so considerable a section of the rugged stalwarts of Labour'. Suddenly the latter, with clouded and puzzled brow, asked abruptly: 'I suppose I'm right in thinking you don't *believe* in those things you're defending against Blatchford?' Assured by

Chesterton that he most certainly did, the scholarly refined face did not move a muscle, yet it completely altered. 'Oh, you *do*,' he replied, 'I beg your pardon. Thank you. That's all I wanted to know'—and from that moment the man who believed in God was obviously looked upon as a fabulous griffin.

The academic gentleman from Cambridge was not Sydney Cockerell. One wishes it had been. Chesterton's, indeed, is a name oddly absent from all the letters S.C.C. wrote to Dame Laurentia. The names which do figure there dazzle and entrance the reader —Ruskin, Tolstoy, Conrad, Hardy, W. B. Yeats, Francis Thompson, Belloc, Shaw, Lawrence of Arabia, John Masefield, Walter de la Mare, to name but a few—yet of G. K. Chesterton, the man who had once studied in the schools of Huxley, Carlyle, Ruskin and Tolstoy, who of all others had trodden in early manhood the same path of scepticism and free-thought as Cockerell himself, there is never a mention.

Within a few months of S.C.C.'s first acquaintance with Stanbrook, Chesterton had taken his favourite propositions one by one, proved their utter irrelevancy, and shattered them in the pages of *Orthodoxy*. Contrary to certain reports at the time of her death, Dame Laurentia neither met nor had any contact with Chesterton. She had a great admiration for him, but it is just possible that in the earlier years of the century she had not even heard of him any more than she had heard of Bernard Shaw. In any case, whether Chesterton's logic would have strengthened her hand and helped her to convince one who was seemingly not open to conviction is doubtful. She was quick to perceive the ring of finality in the letter which acknowledged the receipt of *The Penny Catechism*, and in a single sentence by way of reply, she dismissed apologetics for good. 'Thank you for your letter,' she wrote, 'we will leave our differences alone and wish they did not exist.' For the space of almost thirty years of unclouded friendship that remained, they continued to correspond regularly in letters which discoursed of matters grave and gay, tremendous and trifling, domestic and universal, but never again did either make any further references to the beliefs they could not share.

She had not, however, spoken her final word. Some years later, looking backward over the many yesterdays of their friendship, and at the same time looking forward to that day after tomorrow when, to quote St Thomas More's farewell to his dear, twice-blessed Margaret, they should 'meet together in heaven, there to make merry for ever, and never have trouble after', Dame Laurentia spoke to the man whose friendship she ever considered one of God's greatest gifts to her, in words which may fittingly serve as an epilogue:

'What a gift, and what a mystery, such a beautiful friendship is! May ours grow always into still deeper understanding until we are done with this earthly life, and may we come to perfect comprehension in eternal life, where I firmly believe all that is best and noblest in us will have its fulfilment. I will say what St Oswald of Worcester said when leaving his monks of Ramsey: "Consociet nos Christus in paradiso". Do say *Amen*.'

3

The Nun and the Dramatist

AT THE CLOSE of Vespers on the afternoon of 5 September 1884, an eighteen-year-old girl clad in rich bridal attire knelt on the altar steps in the sanctuary of the church at Stanbrook before the Right Reverend William Clifford, Bishop of Clifton, and the following dialogue took place:

"What do you ask?"
"The mercy of God and the grace of the holy habit."
"Do you ask it with your whole heart?"
"Yes, my Lord, I do."
"May God grant you perseverance, my daughter."

The Bishop then proceeded to shear off her long fair hair. A few minutes later, divested of silks and ornaments and habited in a plain wide-sleeved tunic of rough serge, she once more knelt before him to be formally clothed with a girdle, scapular and white veil symbolizing her official reception into the thirteen-centuries-old Order of St Benedict. The great enclosure door swung open in answer to the novice's importunate knocking, and presently closed slowly again behind her, shutting out the world and its vanities for ever.

On the evening of that same day, in the presence of an earnest group of high-minded socialists met together at 17 Osnaburgh Street, N.W., the house of E. R. Pease, a member of the Society of Psychical Research, a twenty-eight-year-old 'raw aggressive Dubliner', to quote H. G. Wells, 'with a thin flame-coloured beard beneath his white, illuminated face', duly enrolled the name George Bernard Shaw in the official list of membership of the eight-months-old Fabian Society.

Greater contrast can scarcely be imagined than between the girl who withdrew into the fastness of the cloister to live a life of subjection and poverty according to the counsels of the gospel of Christ, and the man who went forth into the world to proclaim a doctrine of justice, brotherhood and equality according to the gospel of Karl Marx. That their paths should ever cross seemed inconceivable.

'My dissipations have begun again,' wrote Sydney Cockerell to Dame Laurentia over twenty years later, 29 May 1907. 'Yesterday at the Bodleian from about 10 till 4. Then to town and supper with Lady D. and with her and her husband to a lecture by Bernard Shaw on "Socialism and the Middle Classes"—and very good it was. I wonder whether G.B.S.'s fame has got as far as Stanbrook, and whether he is there regarded as an imp of the devil—I have known him for many years and regard him not only as one of the cleverest (that is nothing) but as one of the best and honestest of living Englishmen.'

Apparently, however, acquaintance with even the name of Bernard Shaw was an exception to that seeming universality of knowledge of hers which had so struck Sydney Cockerell at their first meeting. 'I have never heard of Mr Bernard Shaw,' she replied, 'but perhaps others in the house have. I don't like to think that a person whom you regard with respect should be to us as a limb of the evil one!'

Sydney Cockerell was one of Bernard Shaw's oldest friends and one of his greatest. He first made his acquaintance in 1889; in 1891 and 1894 he travelled with him in Italy among a party of members of the Art-Workers' Guild; and during the early years of the twentieth century he watched Shaw's growing fame as a dramatist whose brilliant and argumentative dialogue, besides reflecting current problems of science, religion and economics, was also recreating and revolutionizing the English theatre in a manner unknown since the seventeenth century. The Vedrenne-Barker productions of Shaw's most outstanding plays at the Court Theatre between 1904 and 1907 had won European recognition for Shaw's dramatic genius. Although Sydney Cockerell attended every play, he found it difficult to decide whether the nun who had recently rejected Tolstoy would be willing to extend a welcome to any plays, pleasant or unpleasant. He did not put the question to the test, but contented himself with sending her one of the outstanding features of the Court programme, Gilbert Murray's translations of Euripides.

It was neither the socialist reformer, however, nor the dramatist of genius in Shaw, but the man of unimpeachable honesty and integrity who commanded Sydney Cockerell's loyalty and devotion. Feeling by instinct that spirit would answer spirit, it was this man whom he hoped one day to bring into contact with Dame Laurentia. 'Some I have to keep apart,' he had written of his friends in words already quoted, 'others I wish to bring together. There are several I should very much like you to meet.' . . . But how to get one whom all London was lionizing to a tiny parlour in a strictly enclosed convent of nuns in the remote English village of Callow End?

Callow End lies in the broad Severn valley about four miles south of Worcester and a mile from the main route between Worcester and Malvern. With its orchards and hopyards, its slight sprinkling of picturesque half-timbered houses amid a medley of nondescript modern brick dwellings, with its little school, its post office and its two inns, the village straggles along the winding road to Upton-on-Severn and strays off right and left along half-a-dozen lanes, upwards to undulating farm-lands and low round-topped hills on the one side, downwards to the west bank of the Severn, to the flour mill and the disused ferry on the other. In spite of having absorbed its near neighbours, Pixham and Stanbrook, and bestowed upon all the least lovely name of the three, Callow End is in reality no more than an overgrown hamlet, dependent upon the parish of Powick a mile away. It possesses no official entity and no ancient church. Yet one notable landmark Callow End does possess—the pile of Victorian Gothic buildings known as Stanbrook Abbey. Screened from the north by a belt of trees, the Abbey, with its little Puginesque church and its tall, creeper-clad line of frontage, stands on a slight eminence beyond a sloping green meadow at the very entrance of the village, somewhat aloof but clearly visible from the main road which sweeps round in a wide curve below.

What could there be in such a place to attract one who said of himself that his nature was arboreal, and who felt with Dr Johnson that he who was tired of London was tired of life? The primitive horrors of the countryside appalled him: as likely as not he would find the mile-long track from Powick to Callow End 'an oozy quagmire full of liquid gamboge', to use his own highly descriptive phrase. Considerations such as these might have daunted a less resolute spirit than Sydney Cockerell's: they daunted him not at all. One day Bernard Shaw and Dame Laurentia must meet: that was certain.

Love of the countryside would never have drawn Bernard Shaw to Worcestershire; the society of kindred spirits proved to be the magnet that led, early in the 1920's, to his paying a yearly visit to Malvern, where his familiar figure was often to be seen striding over the hills, deep in discussion with Edward Elgar, Sir Granville Bantock and Sir Barry Jackson, and it was to Malvern he repaired after his London triumph in the spring of 1924. On 26 March the New Theatre produced *St Joan*. Even today in the pages of the *Times Literary Supplement* one reads of Bernard Shaw's having written the play 'in a heat of admiration' three years after St Joan's canonization. It is highly probable that the play had been maturing in G.B.S.'s mind for a solid twenty years, ever since the appearance in 1902 of an English translation of the official Latin text of the Saint's trial in 1431 and rehabilitation in 1456. T. Douglas Murray's *Jeanne d'Arc, Maid of Orleans 1429–1431* had fired the imagination and enthusiasm of the socialist-humanist circle that included men— mere pygmies such as S.C.C.—and supermen like Bernard Shaw. Within weeks of their first meeting, S.C.C. had asked Dame Laurentia: 'Do you know the wonderful trial of Joan of Arc (a verbatim account of question & answer) Englished by T. Douglas Murray & published by Heinemann? It is the most wonderful piece of history imaginable, and though the editor is, I think, a Protestant, the book has received high commendation from the Pope.'

Such was S.C.C.'s admiration for the nineteen-year-old 'witch, blasphemer and apostate', who begged only for the consolation of a little wooden cross latched together out of two sticks by an English soldier as the torches set her alight, that he added her to his select band of giants and heroes—to Francis of Assisi, Thomas More and Galileo, to say nothing of Tolstoy, Ruskin, Morris and the Grand Mufti of Egypt. St Joan must have felt thoroughly at home in such masculine company. And when in 1908 and 1911 two daughters were born to Kate and Sydney Cockerell, was it by sheer coincidence that they were given the names of Joan's two phantom voices, Margaret and Katharine?

Cockerell had already known Shaw for twenty years, discussed and been present at all G.B.S.'s dramatic productions, when he asked Dame Laurentia in 1907 whether Shaw's fame had reached her ears. It seems reasonable to assume that T. D. Murray's large and handsome book of 396 pages with 27 illustrations and map, provided G.B.S. with his source material. In itself the story was high drama, and Shaw was a playwright whose business was to write a good play. This he did in 1924. The production of his *St Joan* at the New Theatre, with Sybil Thorndike in the title-role, was discussed everywhere and hailed with delight as a masterpiece. Whether 'Joan the Protestant', Joan the nationalist, Joan the feminist, Joan the pert, attractive, tiresome stereotype are true images of the virgin-saint canonized by the Church in 1920 is a different question, and in one way this did not concern the dramatist. Sydney Cockerell had been present as usual at the first night, but made no comment on it in a letter to Dame Laurentia: he waited for her to make the first move. All unsuspectingly she fell into the trap. 'I hear Bernard Shaw has written a play about St Joan,' she wrote on 28 March. 'Someone told me he said she was the first protestant! An odd kind of protest—she was always appealing to the Pope.'

Immediately he wrote offering to lend her the text of the play: 'I will lend you Shaw's play to read if it would interest you and if you will promise to take great care of it! I should like to make some alterations—but it is a notable achievement I think. . . . *Joan* is not yet published and mine is a very special copy, which I want back as soon as you have read it. Of course you may read it aloud to the nuns if you think it will edify them.'

A fortnight later she returned the book and innocently gave him the opportunity for which he had longed ever since he knew her. The play had pleased her enormously: possibly its author would do likewise.

'I return *St Joan* with very many thanks,' she wrote on April 15; 'it is a wonderful play, reaching in its simplicity (which must have cost much labour) a high degree of art. Joan herself is beautifully portrayed. Like you I should like to make some alterations, though probably not in the same passages. Mr Shaw's aspect of the trial does not please me. But I suppose it was only by presuming right intentions on the part of the court, that he could work in the "Protestant" idea. It doesn't seem historically right to me, and Joan more than once appealed from the court to Rome and a Council. There are gems of wit and wisdom everywhere. "What is the use of commonsense?" for instance, and Joan's "There is danger everywhere except in Heaven." The author is not tender of the English! What could be better than "How can what an Englishman believes be heresy?"'

On the morning of 24 April 1924 Dame Laurentia received a letter from Mrs Shaw formally enclosing two visiting-cards:

MALVERN HOTEL
MALVERN

'To Dame Laurentia McLachlan
'Dear Madam,
    'Our friend Sydney Cockerell has urged us very strongly to call upon you.
    'We feel a little diffident about doing so, and hope you will not think us intrusive. But it would be a great pleasure to see you.
    '"We" of course means my husband and myself!
Yours sincerely,
C. F. Shaw'

Without awaiting a reply, both visitors arrived in the afternoon of the same day. No account of the hour's interview has been recorded but something of the impressions each made on the other may be gleaned from subsequent letters and conversations. The letter Dame Laurentia despatched at once to Sydney Cockerell is disappointing in its brevity and reticence:

'While I was reading your letter yesterday afternoon Mr and

Mrs Shaw were announced, so I was saved the trouble of an alarming prospect by finding myself at once with an un-alarming reality. They were charming, and *St Joan* was discussed, with other subjects, in a very pleasant conversation. I was greatly interested to meet such a famous man, one more privilege for which I have to thank you, and my impression is that we got on very well together. They say they will repeat the visit when they are in Malvern again. Mr Shaw gave good reasons for his treatment of *St Joan*, with regard to the points that I questioned.'

Almost twenty years later she summed up her impression of the man in few but telling words: 'I have just been reading Titterton's *So this is Shaw*, and it confirms the impression made by G.B.S. on my first meeting with him—absolute sincerity and simplicity.'

Dissatisfied with her somewhat laconic report of the meeting he had engineered, and anxious to know whether his strategy had succeeded, Sydney Cockerell wrote a letter reproaching Mrs Shaw for her long silence. He was rewarded with an immediate reply, written on 3 June 1924:

'I quite agree we were perfect *fiends* never to write and thank you for the introduction to Dame Laurentia McLachlan, and to tell you how very greatly we enjoyed our visit to her. We have no excuse except that we left Malvern the next day and went rushing about the country—to Stratford, where we went to plays all day and all night, and to Norwich, where G.B.S. addressed 4,000 people etc. etc. It was horrible of me not to write. We were so greatly interested in and by the lady, and in all her surroundings, for, though I have often been in convents, I have never talked through bars before. We liked her *very* much.'

More illuminating than all else, however, is a brief note, found after Dame Laurentia's death appended to her collection of Bernard Shaw's letters:

'S.C.C. told me that after Shaw's first visit he received an enthusiastic report of it, and he asked Shaw when he was coming again. "Never," said G.B.S. . . . Then he reflected and asked, "How long has she been there?" "Nearly fifty years." "Oh, that alters the case, I'll go whenever I can." He thought I had come in ready made from the world, but when he found that whatever I am is the result of my life here he was impressed. This gives me confidence to hope that God may use me for this soul's salvation. If it were only a matter of his liking me, I should think little of it, but it seems that the life here, and therefore the Church, does attract him. God give me grace to help this poor wanderer so richly gifted by you.'

G.B.S.'s 'Never' proved to be of very short duration, for on 9 July of the same year he was already proposing another visit: 'We are just off for a trip in Scotland (how I wish I were enclosed, and never had to pack or not know at what hotel to lay my head!) and we may return south by way of Worcester, in which case we shall certainly blow in—if that is a proper way to visit an Abbey.' It was during one of his visits at this time that he purchased *The Letters of St Teresa of Avila*, recently translated and printed at Stanbrook. One can only lament that he did not follow up *St Joan* with a play on the great Spanish Carmelite.

A few months later, on 1 October, Shaw made Dame Laurentia a gift of a copy of *St Joan* complete with the preface which as yet she had not seen, since it formed an independent essay, written only in May 1924 some time after the play itself had been produced. 'I am in possession of my own *St Joan*,' she wrote to Sydney Cockerell, 'adorned with the inscription "To Sister Laurentia from Brother Bernard"! Mr Shaw is becoming quite monastic. I have thanked him and said that if I thought I had anything to say after reading the preface, I should ask leave to say it.'

Much of the preface could not but win Dame Laurentia's wholehearted approval. To S.C.C. she wrote on 3 November 1924: 'Our old French chaplain is reading St Joan with great delight and equal wonderment. He is in admiration of Brother Bernard's power, and not a little puzzled by the Preface. To tell the truth, so am I. For the most part I admire and agree, but when it comes to disagreeing, I find judgement very difficult.

Brother Bernard has such a pretty knack of turning on you with a whimsical smile when you think you have caught him.' She was not likely to quarrel with Shaw's assertion that there is no Rationalism so rationalistic as Catholic rationalism. As a Catholic she was as free as he was to believe or disbelieve in private revelations, to which only a purely human or probable authority is attached; and no Catholic should ever be deceived into thinking that the saints and angels of St Joan's or any other saint's visions, clothed in rich garments and visible to the eye in bodies which they do not in reality possess, are anything but symbols whose appearance accords with the ideas of the person who sees them, or those of the painters of his day. One of the greatest visions— that of the four living creatures round about the throne in the Apocalypse—has largely been borrowed by St John from the prophet Ezechiel who himself adapted the image from the gigantic bas-reliefs of the Assyrian palaces familiar to the eyes of every Jew during the Captivity. God transmits his light through the mists of familiar surroundings and individual outlook, and revelations have to be understood in a spiritual sense. It was precisely because St Joan herself took her visions too literally that she misinterpreted their real significance. With so much Dame Laurentia was in agreement. But when Shaw went on to urge that Catholicism was not Catholic enough, since the Church's blunders deter Freethinkers from joining it and a Church which has no place for Freethinkers has neither future in modern culture nor belief in the validity of its own doctrines, Dame Laurentia immediately challenged him to define what he meant by Freethought. She suspected that his freethought was synonymous with false thought—truth alone makes a man free.

She also had an addition to suggest. In the Epilogue to *St Joan* Bernard Shaw in splendid vision saw the Church of 1920, ever old and ever new, proclaiming in the person of a gentleman in morning coat and tall hat the fact of St Joan's canonization in the Vatican Basilica: "On every thirtieth of May, being the anniversary of the death of the said most blessed daughter of God, there shall in every Catholic church to the end of time be celebrated a special office in commemoration of her. . . ."

Dame Laurentia divined that while G.B.S. had diligently studied at first hand the reports of St Joan's trial and rehabilitation, it had never occurred to him to consult the 'special office' of which the gentleman dressed in twentieth-century fashion spoke. The Church's official judgement on St Joan is to be found epitomized and crystallized for ever in the Mass appointed for her feast. Dame Laurentia therefore proceeded to send the passage from the Book of Wisdom selected for the Epistle of the Mass as an example of a succinct and perfect summary of Shaw's analysis of Joan throughout preface and play:

'I purposed to take wisdom to me to live with me: knowing that she will communicate to me of her good things, and be a comfort in my cares and grief. For her sake I shall have glory among the multitude, and honour with the elders, though I be young. And I shall be found of a quick conceit in judgement, and shall be admired in the sight of the mighty, and the faces of princes shall marvel at me. When I hold my peace, they shall wait for me; and when I speak they shall look upon me; and if I talk much, they shall lay their hands on their mouths. Moreover by the means of her I shall have immortality: and shall leave behind me an everlasting memory unto them that come after me. I shall set the people in order: and nations shall be subject unto me. Terrible kings hearing shall fear me; among the multitude I shall be found good, and in war valiant.' (*Wisdom* viii, 9–15.)

Her reply, unfortunately, seems to be lost for ever, but the gist of her letter of thanks for the gift of *St Joan* may be gathered from one she wrote on 2 January 1925 to Sydney Cockerell. Although written after G.B.S.'s letter of 23 December 1924, it is transcribed first in order to appreciate his references:

'The enclosed came on Christmas Day from Brother Bernard— a remarkable letter which pleases me greatly in spite of its heresies. You will be able to follow the points of my letter pretty easily. The first paragraph of the second sheet[1] refers to my remark about the Church's objection to Freethinking. I said that to my mind no thinker was so free as a Catholic— the limitations being in the direction of good sense and ensuring

[1] i.e. Paragraph beginning 'I am quite aware. . . .'

right thinking, that it is not freedom to be able to think contrary to objective truth. As an example of the liberty left to theologians, I mentioned a big discussion going on at present on the nature of the Sacrifice in the Mass. Then I could not resist quoting a remark made to me a few days before by Dom Bouré, the French monk who lives here. Speaking of these things and Protestantism, he said: "Ma Mère, le protestantisme démolit la cervelle"! I thought I could not deprive Brother Bernard of that fine thought. The reference to the Book of Wisdom means that I had referred him to that Book, viii, 9–15, for the passage chosen as a lesson on St Joan's feast. I think you will agree that the choice could scarcely be bettered. I shall not bother Br. B. again, but when he next shakes my bars I shall make some further remarks.'

Her letter to Shaw had been accompanied with a copy of a small book entitled *The Godly Instructions and Prayers of Blessed Thomas More Written in the Tower of London* 1535, recently printed at Stanbrook in preparation for the tercentenary of the monastery's foundation. His reply, the first letter of a series extending over a period of twenty-six years until his death in 1950, is here given in its entirety:

10 ADELPHI TERRACE
LONDON, W.C.2.
23 December 1924

'My dear Sister Laurentia,
'In reading heathen literature like mine you must always allow for the special meaning given by the Church to the word supernatural. Also you must remember that I am addressing an audience not exclusively Catholic, including not only Protestants and Modernists of all sorts, but also Indians and Orientals whose religion has an iconography entirely different to the Christian one. Whether God makes different iconographies for different peoples, or whether He lets us all make our own iconography, it is clear that to a pious Hindoo or Moslem St Michael and St Catherine mean nothing, just as to a Worcester dairymaid Allah and Brahma mean nothing. Christ, in His metaphor of the tares and the wheat, has given

us a very plain warning to let Allah and Brahma and Vishnu alone, as if our rash missionaries pluck them out of the Arab and Hindu soul, they will pluck all the religion out of that soul as well. This explains why missionary converts are usually undesirables.

'It was therefore necessary for me to present Joan's visions in such a way as to make them completely independent of the iconography attached to her religion. But I did not therefore deprive the visions of their miraculous character. If she had been born at the other side of the Ural mountains she would have seen, not St Michael, but Mahomet or Buddha or Vishnu or Lao-tse. She would perhaps have spat at the blessed Michael just as, being what she was, a Western Christian, she would have spat at "the accurst Mahound". God adapts his method of revelation to the powers and faculties and knowledge of his creatures. We cannot, for instance, believe that God would have mocked Joan with a written revelation which she could not read; yet that would not be a more inconsiderate proceeding than sending a messenger in whose existence she did not believe. The divine inspiration takes the path of least resistance; and whether you believe that the messengers are real persons or illusions—and I have to leave this an open question to retain the interest of the modernists, who would otherwise reject the inspiration with the objectivity of the vision in the same violent regurgitation—the inspiration loses none of its divinity either way.

'This does not please the many Catholics who are not really catholic at all, as they cling consciously or unconsciously to the doctrine of exclusive salvation, which carries with it the doctrine of exclusive revelation; but if I wrote in terms of this doctrine I should, from their point of view, be calling, not sinners, but the righteous to salvation; and my book would reach no further than the penny lives of the saints which they sell in the Churches in Ireland. I want my sound to go out into all lands.

'I am quite aware that Catholicism has produced much more audacious philosophic speculation than Protestantism. What is more, there is no Rationalism so rationalistic as Catholic Rationalism. When the monk said that Protestantism destroys the brain I think he meant that Protestantism leads men to break through the limits of reason, just as the mathematicians did when, finding they could get no further with possible quantities, they assumed impossible ones like the square root of minus x. I exhausted rationalism when I got to the end of my second novel at the age of twenty-four, and should have come to a dead stop if I had not proceeded to purely mystical assumptions. I thus perhaps destroyed my brain; but inspiration filled up the void; and I got on better than ever. I suspect that monk's orthodoxy. *Cucullus non facit monachum.*

'I am delighted to learn that my St Joan is yours also. It sets my mind completely at ease: I know now that I have done the trick. The passage from the Book of Wisdom amazed me. For having chosen it may all the sins of the Church be forgiven!

'Thanks for the St Thomas More book, which is excellently printed. Some bits of it are very good; but the Psalm part of it is a mere literary exercise, quite out of character with his personal attitude towards his enemies. To make a clean breast of it to you, I do not like the Psalms: they seem to me to be the classic examples of fool's comfort. Comforting people by telling them what they would like to believe when both parties know that it is not true is sometimes humane, and always to be let off with a light pennance [*sic*] as between two frail mortals; but it should not be admitted to the canon. I like Wisdom ever so much better.

'I must stop, or I shall begin by kicking my cloven hoof too obviously for your dignity and peace; but I mean well, and find great solace in writing to you instead of to all the worldly people whose letters are howling to be answered.

'On the 26th we sail to Madeira for six weeks or thereabouts. When we are next touring in your neighbourhood I shall again shake your bars and look longingly at the freedom at the other side of them.

Faithfully

G. Bernard Shaw'

With reference to the fool's comfort provided by the psalms of which the above letter speaks, it may be worth while to point out that fifteen centuries before Shaw, St Augustine had felt and faced the problem—and being Augustine, had turned the tables very adroitly on the real fool of the piece. 'It is possible,' he says in a sermon on the thirty-sixth psalm, 'that some ill-balanced soul, incapable of understanding the Scriptures in a spiritual way, may be inwardly scandalized, and ask: Is what I have chanted really true? Is it really true—as I have stood in church singing forth in such pious tones—that *I have never seen the just forsaken, nor his seed seeking bread*? The Scriptures play us false.' To such 'a narrow-minded simpleton if nothing worse' St Augustine has only one reply: 'You must strip off the outer covering and penetrate to our Lord, for if you are captious and crafty and everlastingly bent on picking holes in the basket that contains it, you may never attain to tasting the bread.'

But if Bernard Shaw was deaf to the appeal of the psalms, he showed himself surprisingly alive to the implications of the contemplative life and to the freedom paradoxically symbolized by the double iron grille. Chesterton said of him: 'There is always something about him which suggests that in a sweeter and more solid civilization he would have been a great saint. He would have been a saint of a sternly ascetic, perhaps of a sternly negative type. But he has this strange note of the saint in him: that he is literally unworldly.' Indeed, one is led to wonder how far the man who discarded the George of his Christian name, and became the Brother Bernard of Dame Laurentia's letters, was secretly influenced by admiration for his namesake, the Abbot of Clairvaux, in his choice of a vegetarian regime Cistercian in its austerity, his love of our Lady, and the government of his thought by what he termed 'mystical assumptions'. The coolness and effrontery originating from his extreme shyness, the love of shocking lion-hunters with outrageous remarks, and—most Irish of all his traits—the levity with which he disguised his deepest feelings, found no place before Dame Laurentia. Brilliant, disconcerting and dynamic he could not help being, yet his fundamental humility, tact and quick understanding became more and more apparent in his relations with her as the years passed. When the Malvern Festival was inaugurated in 1929 with the production of *The Apple Cart*, Sydney Cockerell accompanied Shaw on one of his visits to Stanbrook on 22 August, and confessed that on that occasion he saw a G.B.S. almost unknown to him. 'I never saw him so abashed by anyone but William Morris,' he remarked many years later to a member of the community. 'With Morris and your dear Abbess he was on his good behaviour and seemed to admit that he was in the presence of a being superior to himself.'

On this occasion the two men paid a morning call on Dame Laurentia, after which Shaw returned to Malvern, leaving S.C.C. to a tête-à-tête with her in the afternoon. 'Yesterday was indeed a memorable day,' he wrote on the 23rd. 'I don't know whether I most enjoyed the morning or the afternoon. It was an immense treat to see you and Shaw together. You were both at your best & I think the encounter was a mutual tonic.' To this she replied: 'Yes, Thursday was a great occasion. Brother Bernard was delicious enough to deserve half an hour out of your day. . . . I have read "The Apple Cart" with great delight. What dialogue! Act II interested me very much. Edith Craig had explained to me its autobiographical significance, and under the cold-&-clear-as-ice brain, I found a good deal of emotion in his treatment of the eternal problem.' The next letter strikes a strange note that must surely have been mere fun. In November she wrote: 'I feel strongly inclined to take Brother Bernard's advice and sell the valuable copy of "The Apple Cart" enriched with his autograph. How does one set about such things without exposing oneself to the danger of a headline: "G.B.S. and his nun-friend"?' This evoked a Cockerellian *mot juste*: 'I think you must keep "The Apple Cart". After you have both been canonized it will be far more valuable & the headlines won't matter.'

On 24 September 1930 Shaw paid an unexpected visit to Stanbrook, only to find that Dame Laurentia was ill and could not see him. He was received by a junior nun Dame Anne Dowson who, as a sometime member of Lena Ashwell's group, had a good working knowledge of the theatre. To an S.C.C. wringing his hands at his inability to prevent her wasting her life by passing from stage to cloister, she had written: 'I am not being in any way pressed to stay, rather the reverse. The only person I feel that wishes me to stay is God. Possibly that sounds nonsense, but it is the same sort of knowledge you have about right and wrong, conscience really. . . . There was a moment in the Theatre when I knew that if I liked to push myself the smallest bit I could have had a good job and a lasting one, and I could not make the move. It was not worth my life, I felt.' After Shaw's visit, she reported to S.C.C.: 'I felt like an inadequate understudy going on without announcement in place of a star when I went down to Bernard Shaw. But his perfect manners saved me any discomfort. And I did enjoy my few minutes' talk.' Next day Shaw wrote to Dame Laurentia from Whitehall Court:

'I am greatly concerned lest I should have "put a thought" on you yesterday. I was wondering whether I should not break in on you at the wrong moment, as your duties and devotions must be many. And suddenly came the thought that you might be ill. As far as I can guess, it was at about that unlucky moment that you felt ill and went to bed. But if I was the active party in the transaction you must have recovered instantly and violently; for all my wishes and whatever corresponds in a heathen like me to prayers have set with an overwhelming tide in that direction since your . . . understudy told me what had happened. But I prefer to believe that you were the telepathist and I the recipient. Make them tell me how you are; for there are so few people in the world that matter particularly that, being old (75) and selfish, I cannot refrain from selfishly crying "Abstain thee from felicity awhile." I do not think Christopher St John is in any worse plight than usual. You must not be disturbed when you hear that literary and theatrical people are on the rocks: they *live* there. I heard from her the other day about those letters of Ellen Terry's and mine. They raise the question of the publication of the letters; and I shrink from it; and you say No; and Colonel Lawrence (ex-prince of Damascus) says No. And then, I hear that the whole budget of letters has been sold to an American speculator for several thousand pounds, which he declares he paid on the understanding that he might publish them! What can you do but pray for us all?

'I fancy some meddlesome saint or other has made you ill to make your friends feel how much your friendship means to them. As the trick has succeeded terribly well in my case, please send your understudy to pray to St Meddlesome to drop it. Ever your Brother Bernard.'

In March 1931 Shaw joined a party of pilgrims to the Holy Land, Egypt and Italy. As prelude to his departure, Dame Laurentia sent a letter to wish him godspeed and ask for some tiny souvenir:

1 March 1931

'Dear Brother Bernard,

'Before you start for the Holy Land I want to send you my blessing and ask you to take me, my spirit, with you, and let it run about in the Holy Places which I know without having seen them. Will you lay my love and reverence at Our Lord's feet in that wonderful land, and bring me back some little trifle from Calvary? I shall be thinking of you and the other pilgrims and I shall know when you return, for among the company is Miss Martineau, a cousin of our Dame Anne's, the nun whom you saw in September.

'A good and happy pilgrimage to you and Mrs Shaw, from your

Sister Laurentia.'

Mildred Martineau sent Dame Anne regular bulletins in which their most famous pilgrim of course figures largely. 'She was very much struck by his kindness and affability to all,' Dame Anne wrote to S.C.C. 'Also she told me of a wonderful lecture he gave them. She enjoyed the whole thing enormously.' Yet in the midst of all the adulation and the comings and goings, G.B.S. found time to send Dame Laurentia a few leaves from the Garden of Gethsemane with his assurance:

HOTEL FAST, JERUSALEM
15 March 1931

'Dear Sister Laurentia,

'Just a hurried line in the middle of my packing as I leave Jerusalem for Nazareth.

'Later on I will write fully about my pilgrimage and the extraordinary difficulty in finding a real relic for you in this City of Destruction where relics are thrust on you for sale (by Jews) at every corner.

'I shall not get back to the ship until Thursday the 19th.

Then, if the sea is propitious, I shall have time to write.

'Meanwhile the enclosed leaves are real as far as they go.

affectionately

G.B.S. (Fr Bernardo).

'I shall be at the Grand Hotel, Venice, on the 1st April for some days.'

She took the hint implied in his postscript, and on 27 March sent a letter of acknowledgement to the Grand Hotel, Venice, to await his arrival:

'Thank you very much for your note and the precious little souvenirs of Gethsemane. That olive-grove must be one of the most interesting spots in the Holy Land. I look forward to the promised account of your pilgrimage. I have often thought that I could scarcely bear to visit the Holy Land under modern conditions, but this is probably foolish, for one ought to be able to discount undesirable surroundings, and people, and get down to the Palestine that Christ sanctified. I wonder how you feel about it.

'Christopher [St John] tells me that *the* Letters are coming out. From your letter in September I gathered that you had no choice left in the matter. At any rate their appearance brings great contentment to Bedford St., and your generosity a certain ease for which I am very thankful. I hope Christopher will now be free to use her talent to some purpose.

'Thank you again for thinking of me in your travels.'

The trip to Venice in 1931 must have cost Shaw considerably more than when he first made it in 1891 in the company of twenty-seven members of the Art-Workers' Guild, at an inclusive price of thirteen pounds, ten shillings for a holiday of twelve days. He then considered that the exterior of St Mark's would have been 'ideal for a railway station' and far from appraising the beauty of churches, palaces and pictures, he dwelt in his long letter to William Morris on the desirability of perspiring so freely as to give fleas rheumatism, a hideously unpleasant complaint for an insect that has to jump for its life every few seconds. One may regret, but perhaps it is just as well, that he

100

had already discharged the debt of the letter he had promised Dame Laurentia. He had not waited until he re-embarked, but two days after sending the olive leaves he splendidly fulfilled his promise to send a full account of his pilgrimage. Accompanied by three snapshots of Jerusalem and Nazareth not too happily focused, and by a portrait of the writer on board ship with his fellow-traveller Dean Inge, subscribed: 'The Temptation: The Devil and the Dean of St Paul's. Marseilles. 4 March 1931', the letter, written on green paper selected presumably in honour of St Patrick, occupies thirteen sheets roughly nine inches by six inches in measurement. As the chief record of Bernard Shaw's impressions of his tour throughout the Holy Land, this very personal document, a masterpiece of exact observation from start to finish, deserves careful attention. It abounds in felicities of thought and expression, in descriptions so telling yet seemingly so spontaneous as to indicate consummate art, and in shrewd epigrams flung out casually as he goes along. One marvels, to take but one instance, at the ease with which he sums up the very essence of a religious vocation and tosses off in a single neat phrase the age-long contention between protagonists of the active and contemplative life, Martha versus Mary—'girls whom you might enlist for Stanbrook without expecting them to excel in doing as well as in being'.

Such a perfectly sincere letter strives after no effect, yet is notably pervaded with an extraordinary feeling for Christian tradition. The writer shows himself as sensitive to visual impressions and religious emotions as the most orthodox could wish. At one moment the sight of a boy or young man dressed in the fashion of the East recalls our Lord's journeyings; at another, 'the appearance of a woman with an infant in her arms takes on the quality of a vision'. His reactions to the Lake of Tiberias and his shattering of the shrines will find a response in the mind of many a believer. 'There is no land on earth,' he concludes, 'quite like it.'

Yet the letter bears evidence of inward conflict. The reader is sometimes touchingly reminded of St Paul's words to the Athenians regarding God's purpose in creating the human race, 'that they should seek God, if haply groping after him they might find him'. In a significant passage, Shaw relates how as he stood on Mount Olivet on the traditional spot of our Lord's Ascension into heaven, his ultra-logical intellect warred against his religious instincts. Unconsciously, perhaps, the man who set such store by 'mystical assumptions' would have been glad to believe, but the fierce logician in him could not become a humble child and accept faith when he met it. It must of course be remembered that he was in the company of Dean Inge, who to the very year of his death used to contribute a column to the daily press at the feast of our Lord's Ascension protesting against the ridiculous impossibility of any soaring into the empyrean as if the sky were the dome of earth and the floor of heaven. One wonders whether the authority on Plotinus and the Bampton lecturer on Mysticism had never read the fourteenth-century masterpiece, *The Cloud of Unknowing*.

'Since it so was that Christ should ascend bodily, and thereafter send the Holy Ghost bodily, therefore it was more seemly that it was upwards and from above than either downwards and from beneath, behind, or before, on one side or on other. But else than for this seemliness, he needed never the more to have gone upwards than downwards; I mean for nearness of the way. For heaven ghostly is as near down as up, and up as down, behind as before, before as behind, on one side as on other. For the high and the nearest way thither is run by desires, and not by paces of feet.' (*The Cloud of Unknowing*, Chap. 60.)

Discussing the Ascension and the authorship of the Apocalypse Bernard Shaw shows himself as following Dean Inge's lead. He accordingly meets the *mysterium continuum* of the Sacred Books in which all the great symbols of the Old Testament are caught up in Christ and carried into eternity, with the unscholarly and irreverent negations of the then prevailing school of Higher Criticism. The dramatist who created St Joan in the great European and Christian tradition, and the pilgrim in the Holy Land whose soul thrilled in glad response to the sight of a mother with her babe at Bethlehem, is surely the truer and the greater Bernard Shaw.

St Patrick's Day in Damascus 1931

'Dear Sister Laurentia,

'This Holy Land is in a queer situation from the Crusaders' point of view, which is officially your point of view. The British representative in Jerusalem is also the representative, precisely, of Pontius Pilate; and when Communist Messiahs turn up, as they actually do from time to time under Russian influences, he is bound to handle the case on Pilatical lines. What would any medieval Christian saint—or say Richard Cœur de Lion—say if miraculously resuscitated in Jerusalem today? Saladin and the followers of the accurst Mahound vanquished at last by the Christian British Empire. The circumcised crucifiers of Christ scattered through the ghettos of Europe. The Cross triumphant over all the Promised Land, over Christ's birthplace, over his sepulchre, over the Mount of the Beatitudes and over the bloodstained plain (which Christ overlooked from that Mount) on which Saladin smashed the last effort of the Crusaders to resist him, over Galilee and Samaria, Bethlehem, Nazareth, Capernaum, over the waters on which he walked and the hillsides from which he preached, over Nain and Cana and Bethany, over Jordan in which he was baptized, and the unknown Golgotha on which he was duly executed according to the official routine by the predecessor of Mr Keith Roach.

'So far, praised be God, Richard would say, probably adding a stentorian Hep, hep, hep!

'But when Richard was further informed that the use England had made of its victory was to hand over all that sacred territory to the descendants and co-religionists of Saladin and to those of Annas and Caiphas, having promised it to both for their help in the war, and that Pontius now had his hands full with the job of keeping the peace between them, he would surely either start a new crusade or return to his tomb in disgust with a world gone entirely mad.

'I ask myself whether I shall persuade Sister Laurentia to get a hundred days indulgence, a tailormade short skirt, gaiter boots, a Fair Isle pullover, a smart waterproof, a field glass and camera, a brown sun umbrella lined with red, and a Revelation suitcase, and hasten hither to see for herself what she has imagined at Stanbrook. I leave the question unanswered; but I will tell you what might happen to you because it has happened to me.

'You would enter the Holy Land at night under a strong impression made on you in Egypt, not by the Tutankhamen trash which the tourists are now mobbing, but by something seen under the pyramids. A pyramid is just as big as its royal builder is old; and it is always finished. If he dies a baby, there is his monument ready for him, like this: △ . If he grows up,

his tomb grows with him △ △ △ and so on, if he lives

as long as Cheops, to △ . There was a redhaired queen who

made a tomb for herself and her daughters, deep under tons of pyramid and rock, and set two great artists, Rahay a painter and Yenkaf a sculptor, to work in it. Whether the redhaired one and her brood were very fine ladies, or whether the two fine artists made fine ladies of them I do not know; but when you see that row of sculptured women come alive in a hundred candle power electric sunlight without a shadow of death or fear on their shining faces and pleasantly courteous eyes or a line or contour in their whole bodies that is not exquisite, and when you turn to their magnificently designed portraits on the wall, the impression you receive is beyond description in our lower language, as of an order of beings completely redeemed from sin and vulgarity and all the plagues of our degradation, and yet not in the least geniuses, as Michael Angelo would have made them, but girls whom you might enlist for Stanbrook without expecting them to excel in doing as well as in being. You might question their vocation on the ground that they seem to have no religion nor to need any, having achieved excellence and being content to leave it at that; but the impression would be all the more astonishing. And that to those who served them fifty tons of solid stone seemed as easy to move and handle as a little water in a spoon, gets far beyond our miracles which are wondered at as miracles and taken as divine testimonies, and lifts us into a region in which the miraculous is no longer miraculous but gigantically normal, and immortality a thing to be achieved in a turn of the hand.

'Under such impressions you find yourself in the Holy Land by night, with strange new constellations all over the sky and the old ones all topsy turvy, but with the stars soft and large and down quite close overhead in a sky which you feel to be of a deep and lovely blue. When the light comes you have left the land of Egypt with its endlessly flat Delta utterly behind, and are in a hilly country, with patches of cultivation wrested from the omnipresent stones, which you instantly recognize with a strange emotion which intensifies when you see a small boy coming down one of the patches, and presently, when he has passed away, a bigger boy of about thirteen, beginning to think, and at last, when he too has vanished, a young man, very grave and somewhat troubled, all three being dressed just as Christ dressed. (Here I break off, to resume on the night of the 20th, between Cyprus and Rhodes, at sea.) The appearance of a woman with an infant in her arms takes on the quality of a vision. On this first hour you do not improve. It gives you the feeling that here Christ lived and grew up, and that here Mary bore him and reared him, and that there is no land on earth quite like it.

'Later on the guides try to be more exact. This, they tell you, is the stable in the inn. This is the carpenter's shop. This is the upper chamber where the Last Supper was served. You know that they are romancing—that there is not a scrap of evidence for the possible identifications and that no inn or stable ever existed in a natural cavern in the limestone rock without light or fresh air. In Nazareth you know that Mary used the well in the street because there was (and is) no other well in the town to use; but the water she drew is gone, and the new water, with taps affixed by the British mandatory Government, is anybody's and everybody's water. Everything else in Nazareth except its natural beauty as a hill town is a fraud, meanly commemorated by an unattractive and unimpressive church. But for these frauds every stone in Nazareth would be sacred with possibilities. Because one muddy bend of the Jordan is labelled as the spot on which the dove descended, the whole river is desecrated to make trade for the stall that sells the mud in bottles. I swam in the lake of Tiberias with a pleasant sense that this, at least, was Christ's lake on which nobody could stake out the track on which he walked or the site from which the miraculous draught of fishes was hauled. It is better to have Christ everywhere than somewhere, especially somewhere where he probably wasnt.

'The hills rise almost into mountains over the train to Jerusalem, which winds between them so sinuously that you can see its tail from the window. When you arrive you are surprised: the place has a flourishing modern suburban air, and the new fashionable villa-land is mentioned as The New Jerusalem. When your very modern hotel has completed your disenchantment you make for the old Jerusalem and the church of the Holy Sepulchre. And the only possible comment on it is that of Dean Inge (he is with us on this trip), "Why seek ye the living among the dead? He is not here." (When Dean Inge says the right thing it is so very right that he is privileged to say a hundred wrong things that dont matter.) A sort of case can be made for the sepulchre: it is at least possible that what remains of the chamber in the rock after its smashing up by the Moslem persecutions may be the family vault of Joseph of Arimathea; but when on the same floor a few yards off they shew you Calvary (not a hill) with the sockets of the three crosses, it is irresistibly revealed to you that Saint Helena was a humbug who, when the court was ordered to turn Christian, was quite determined to outshine the Queen of Heaven by a galaxy of visions and miracles that would show the world that Roman queens would enter the new temples as goddesses and not as Syrian peasants cradling their infants in mangers. I know that sort of woman almost as well as you must. I have seen her court in the mosaics of Ravenna, where the attempt of the imperial court ladies to look pious is ludicrously unsuccessful.

'The church of the Holy Sepulchre, to eyes accustomed to western architecture of the same period, is a second rate affair; and the squabbles of the sects over their "rights" in it are not edifying. I duly squeezed myself into the sepulchre, and tipped the queerly robed priest who touched my hands with oil to the extent of five piastres, looking as credulous as I could so as not to hurt his feelings; but my thought was that you would be disappointed. For the rest of the day I damned Jerusalem up hill and down dale; and when they took me to the Mount of Olives (practically oliveless) and showed me the famous view of the city my only comment was "Just like Buxton". But one's appreciation is more complex than that. When you stand on the stone from which the Ascension took place you feel at the same moment everything that the legend means you to feel and a purely comic amusement at the notion of Jesus going up to the highest attainable point as a taking-off place for his celestial flight. Your faith and your tourist's observation jostle one another in the queerest fashion.

'Next day I discovered Jerusalem. I went to the great plain of stone on which the Temple stood, and on which the Mosque of Omar (who didnt build it) stands. And there I found the charm and sanctity of Jerusalem. Christ has been worshipped in both the mosques; Omar was a man after God's own heart; and Mahomet's horse sprang to heaven with him from the great rock which the mosque of Omar enshrines, and which is a nobly beautiful building in spite of the utterly anachronistic Corinthian capitals of the red pillars of granite which bother one all over the Holy Land, and which are so Roman and common. The Kaiser gilt the Corinthian heavily so that they might hit you harder in the eye. Mahomet respected Christ and taught his followers to do the same; and it is perhaps the failure of the Christians to respect Mahomet equally that makes Islam and Israel more impressive in the east than Christendom. Still, the history of the place is such a record of iconoclasms, massacres, persecutions, spoliations, demolitions, and delendings (in Cato's sense) by Turks, Romans, and any conqueror who happened to come along, that the only general verdict possible is that of the King of Brobdingnag. God must feel sick when he looks at Jerusalem. I fancy he consoles himself by turning to Stanbrook.

'You asked me for a relic from Calvary. But St Helena's Calvary is only a spot on a church pavement, jealously guarded, and with nothing removable about it. Where the real Calvary is nobody knows; for the hills outside the city are innumerable. The alleged Via Dolorosa I traversed in a motor-car hooting furiously at the children to get out of the way. The praetorium can be reasonably identified as in the palace of Herod, which Titus kept as a fortress for his garrison when he as nearly as possible left not one stone on another of the rest of the city; but as you cannot tell where Calvary was you cannot tell the way from the praetorium to it.

'So off I went to Bethlehem, a beautifully situated hill town; and from the threshold of the Church of the Nativity I picked up a little stone, a scrap of the limestone rock which certainly existed when the feet of Jesus pattered about on it and the feet of Mary pursued him to keep him in order; for he was a most inconsiderate boy when his family was concerned, as you would realize if you travelled over the distance (at least a day's journey without a Rolls Royce) his mother had to go back to look for him when he gave her the slip to stay and argue with the doctors of divinity. In fact I picked up two little stones: one to be thrown blindfold among the others in Stanbrook garden so that there may always be a stone from Bethlehem there, though nobody will know which it is and be tempted to steal it, and the other for your own self. You shall have them when I return, unless I perish on the way, in which case I shall present myself at the heavenly gate with a stone in each hand, and St Peter will stand at attention and salute the stones (incidentally saluting ME) when he has unlocked the gate and flung it open before me. At least he would if it were ever locked, which I dont believe.

'I have been writing all this in scraps; but there must be an end to everything, even to a letter to you; besides, I finished with the Holy Land at Patmos three days ago, the intervening two days having been spent among heathen idols in and around Athens. For climbing up that frightfully stony road to the top of the mountain where the Greek monastery stands I shall claim indulgence for every sin I ever committed and a few hundred which I still hope to commit. The man who wrote the Book of Revelations, who was *not* the John of the fourth gospel (the Dean assures me that his Greek was disgracefully un-grammatical), ought to have married St Helena. I *know* he was a drug addict, as all the wickednesses of which he accuses God, all the imaginary horrors, all the passings of a thousand years in a second and the visions of universes breaking into three pieces, are the regular symptoms of drug action and delirium tremens. The book is a disgrace to the Bible and should never have been admitted to the canon.

'I began this on the 7th March and it is now the 26th! You can spend a week of your scanty leisure in reading it, and then sell the manuscript to Cockerell for the Fitzwilliam and endow a chapel to St Bernard at Stanbrook with the proceeds. The writing of it has been very restful to the soul of your brother affectionately

G. Bernard Shaw'

In the eyes of its recipient the brilliance of Shaw's letter was its least merit: she valued it rather as a revelation of the true G.B.S.—the idealist with a soul of virginity and violence, as Chesterton had said of his friend, expressing his reactions with ruthless realism. Dame Laurentia considered his criticisms justified—'such as I should have made myself if I had been there'—his appreciations sincere and apt, his tenderness deeply moving. She acknowledged his letter almost immediately:

18 April 1931

'I am so impatient to answer your splendid letter, that I can no longer await the arrival of my precious stones from Bethlehem (the sign of your return) and must at any rate begin today. I recognize of course that any answer or thanks must be utterly inadequate (but that is your fault), and perhaps I ought just to say: "Thank you very much for your nice letter", and leave it at that. But your reflexions are so provocative of thought, that I must say a little more.

'You have made me feel that I have seen the Holy Land through your eyes, and have revealed a great deal more than I should have seen with my own. I have therefore decided not to procure the attractive outfit you describe, and to continue to view the world from my cell at Stanbrook.

'I am not at all troubled to think that the most sacred spots in the Holy Land cannot be identified; quite the contrary. It seems to me "truly right and just", as the Preface of the Mass says, that the sites of such great happenings cannot confidently be recognized. It would hurt much more if Christ were, so to say, localized in Palestine,—if there were a Christian Mecca. "The earth is the Lord's", and he is everywhere spiritually but most truly accessible. Were not the Crusaders to blame for some of the identifications? But if they had not done it, some-one would even now, for this childish mania for labelling everything seems to be universal. I remember hearing a friend say after a second visit to Monte Cassino that on his first visit he had found St Benedict everywhere, whereas a later generation had ticketed the sites of various miracles and events, and thereby had made the place much less impressive. Yet to be in the Holy Land, whatever the drawbacks, and see with your bodily eyes the landscape that Our Lord saw, and swim in his lake, must be a very blessed thing, and I am thrilled by being allowed to share your experience so fully. The modern Jerusalem I should like to forget, especially the part being played by Britain. What must Lawrence think of it all? Above all, what must God think?

'If Christianity is less impressive in the East than Islam, do you not think that is at least partly due to the conditions under which it has existed during Moslem domination? All oppressed religions are in danger of losing something of their external dignity,—look at Catholicism in England and Ireland—besides Latin Catholicism in Palestine is largely represented by Franciscans who are more devotional than liturgical, and who do not abound in taste.

'*April 21.* Your letter has come and the little souvenir of St Francis. I had never heard of that islet. Your young Franciscan has a very capable Guardian Angel! Which reminds me that I have not thanked you for the photographs from the Holy Land. Whatever were the faults of your camera, Gethsemane is just right in its darkness.

'As to the "Temptation" photograph, you will allow me to say that I much prefer the Devil to the Dean!

'*27th.* But this is more than enough, and I must end, awaiting the arrival of my precious stones.

'With much gratitude,

Yours affectionately,

Sister Laurentia.

'P.S. The Fitzwilliam is not going to have your letter, but I have been very nice and allowed S.C.C. to read it. It is well for you that you do not live in the Middle Ages. You would have been boiled in a cauldron of oil for your remarks on the Apocalypse!'

On 12 June he forwarded one of the two stones to which his letter refers with the cryptic remark: 'This is for the garden. Your particular one will come later: the delay is not *my* fault; and the explanation will be satisfactory.'

Meanwhile Dame Laurentia was ill and the doctor had ordered complete rest. In September a letter arrived to ask her if she were free to receive a visit, as the Shaws were in Malvern for the Festival:

18 September 1931

'We must return to London on Tuesday. Could you receive us tomorrow (Saturday) sometime round about four o'clock. We have to lunch in Cheltenham, and, leaving about three, can get to Stanbrook easily before four, or thereafter at any hour that may be convenient to you up to six.

'Failing tomorrow we have Sunday and Monday. The early afternoon between two and three would be best for us on Sunday, or any mortal time on Monday.

'Unless your unenclosed lady who opens the door for me telephones to the contrary before twelve tomorrow, we will call on our way back from Cheltenham. If at that moment you are tired and cannot bear us, it will not upset any of our arrangements: it will only shatter my hopes.

'I have just been in Russia—the oddest place you can imagine. They have thrown God out by the door; and he has come in again by all the windows in the shape of the most tremendous Catholicism.

'I hope they strapped you down in bed and kept the door locked until your overwork had been cured by a spell of thorough laziness.

Your affectionate Brother
Bernard'

111

On the Saturday appointed, Mr and Mrs Shaw arrived bearing with them the stone from Bethlehem intended to serve as Dame Laurentia's personal memento. To her delighted amazement she was presented with an exquisite example of the silversmith's art, almost a foot in height, constructed on the model of a mediaeval reliquary and cunningly devised to focus attention upon the small object enshrined, for which its own beauty is but a setting. It is the work of Paul Cooper, and consists of a chalice-like base decorated with conventional designs of alternate vine-leaves and bunches of grapes in repoussé work, surmounted by a conical imbricated canopy supported on four slender columns, in the midst of which rests a piece of rock of irregular shape measuring about an inch across. On the summit stands a haloed figure of the holy Child, left hand supporting the globe, right hand raised in blessing.

Dame Laurentia was enchanted with the beauty of the gift, and a fortnight later showed it to Sydney Cockerell who paid a visit to reassure himself of her recovery from a really dangerous illness. Noticing that it lacked any mark of its donor's identity, he suggested that it should bear an inscription to indicate its origin. Dame Laurentia accordingly wrote and asked Bernard Shaw to supply a text:

12 October 1931

'Dear Brother Bernard,

'I want to tell you how much the beautiful reliquary is admired and appreciated by Lady Abbess and all the nuns. You know by making such a gift to a place like this you expose yourself to the danger of being prayed for very earnestly. I don't think you will be like the person who retorted, when a friend promised to pray for him, that he would have none of those underhand ways. You have made yourself our debtor and you must take the consequences. Mr Cockerell, who was here last week, was greatly impressed by Paul Cooper's work. He missed only one thing, an inscription saying it was from you to me and explaining its purpose. I had thought of that already. I said we would see to that, but on reflection I think it is your business, or rather your right. Shall we wait till you come again?

'It was such a pleasure to have that talk with you and to see Mrs Shaw again. Please remember me to her.

Your affectionate

Sister Laurentia'

Shaw's reaction to this letter found expression in a yell of execration subsiding into a strangely moving petition:

4, WHITEHALL COURT, LONDON, S.W.1
AYOT ST LAWRENCE, WELWYN, HERTS
25 Oct 1931

'Dear Sister Laurentia

'Cockerell is a heathen atheist: a reliquary is no more to him than a football cup.

'Why can it not be a secret between us and Our Lady and her little boy?

'What the devil—saving your cloth—could we put on it?

'Cockerell writes a good hand. Get him a nice bit of parchment and let him inscribe it with a record of the circumstances for the Abbey archives, if he must provide gossip for antiquarian posterity.

'We couldn't put our names on it—could we? It seems to me something perfectly awful.

'"An inscription explaining its purpose"! If we could explain its purpose we could explain the universe. I couldn't. Could you? If Cockerell thinks he can—and he's quite capable of it—let him try, and submit the result to the Pope.

'Dear Sister: our finger prints are on it, and Heaven knows whose footprints may be on the stone. Isn't that enough?

'Or am I all wrong about it?

faithfully and fraternally
Brother Bernard

'P.S. I don't mind being prayed for. When I play with my wireless set I realize that all the sounds in the world are in my room; for I catch them as I alter the wave length receiver—German, French, Italian and unknown tongues. The ether is full of prayers too; and I suppose if I were God I could tune in to them all. Nobody can tell what influence these prayers have. If the ether is full of impulses of good will to me so much the

113

better for me: it would be shockingly unscientific to doubt it. So let the sisters give me all the prayers they can spare; and don't forget me in yours.'

Was Shaw in this letter merely practising his favourite art of fencing? His attitude to prayer was a dark continent in his complex character. To be flippant and aggressive was part of the image: he was prepared to pounce upon clichés in every department of life, and institutional religion can produce more than its fair share. Yet in 1910, speaking before a packed audience in Reading Town Hall, G.B.S. ended a speech of impassioned sincerity: 'At least I hope so to live that when I'm called before my Maker, if a God there be, I can demand of Him "Give me now my due"'—a statement received with tumultuous applause. At any rate, he had his way with the Bethlehem stone, and did not refuse the consequences of making such a gift to the nun who plagued him with her prayers, as her letter warned him:

30 October 1931

'Dear Brother Bernard,

'You have settled the matter, and there shall be no profaning inscription. A record shall be kept in some other way that will keep your memory green without offending your sense of the fitness of things. Your beautiful gift shall be our secret with Those in whose honour it is made, and the prayers will continue. Do you know I began to pray for you long before I ever saw your face? I then called you (to the Lord) "Bernard Shaw", but now you are "Brother Bernard".

'I am a little in need of prayers myself, since the doctor yesterday found me a little less well and my slight activities are being curtailed. But I must not complain, for these things are slow in mending.

Yours affectionately

Sister Laurentia

'Your address is attractive to a client of St Laurence's. I suppose you have an old church dedicated to him?'

To this day, the little Bethlehem stone, resting on its tiny red cushion amid its silver splendour, bears no indication whatsoever of its origin.

On 8 November, scarcely a week after her letter to Shaw, Dame Laurentia sent S.C.C. a postcard, which read: 'Lady Abbess died yesterday morning. We lay her to rest on Tuesday.' By return of post he replied: 'I am conscious of an element of exultation when a human being departs after a long life so worthily lived. And I think that in the Community there must be mingled feelings of the same kind. I shall always remember her as a very gracious personage who governed the Abbey wisely and broadmindedly and welcomed me with kindness.

'When you receive this the last rites will be over. I do not know whether they are followed by an election, or whether this is postponed for a while. I take it that there can be only one choice, and that with acclamation. And perhaps the burden on your shoulder will be no greater than before.'

His prediction was verified. On 24 November 1931 Dame Anne wrote to inform him: 'R. Mother Prioress was elected Abbess this morning. Everyone seems so happy and it is a most lovely day. You may imagine how glad I am . . . I know you will rejoice with us.' A couple of weeks later she sent him a detailed account, concluding:

'I had a most entertaining letter from Mr Shaw. I wrote to tell him the news & he most kindly wrote to me. I long to show it to you. I would like him to know how much I appreciate his kindness in amusing me. So if you should write to him do tell him how very much I enjoyed his letter. I do not like to trouble him myself.'

The 'most entertaining letter' consisted of a large buff-coloured electioneering poster of five imaginary candidates canvassing for the coveted office of Abbess, drawn up with impish delight in red ink, and sent direct to Dame Anne by way of thanks:

AYOT ST LAWRENCE, WELWYN, HERTS
29 Nov 1931

'Dear Sister Anne,

'Hooray!!!!!!! I didnt dare to write until I knew the result. Thank you most heartily for letting me know. I shall write to

the Lady Abbess when I have a serious moment free.
What is an enclosed election like? This is my notion of it.

BEWARE	VOTE FOR	VOTE FOR
OF	THAT OLD AND TRIED	SR SULPICIA
SHAVIANS	FRIEND	AND
DISGUISED	OF	SHORT
AS	THE ENCLOSED	PRAYERS
BENEDICTINES	DAME LAURENTIA	
VOTE FOR	AND	SISTER
SR DIEHARD	BREAKFAST	ANN
AND	IN	STANDS
BREAD &	BED	FOR
WATER.	THREE	CUTLETS
MORTIFY	TIMES	ON
MORTIFY	A WEEK	FRIDAY
MORTIFY		VERB. SAP.

ROLL UP IN YOUR THOUSANDS TO VOTE
FOR
SISTER MAGDALEN
FORMERLY OF HOLLYWOOD
THE REFORMED VAMP
SNATCH THE BRAND FROM THE BURNING

'Is it really like it?

fraternally

G. Bernard Shaw

Thenceforth, it would have been pleasant to record an ever-deepening and unchequered friendship. Such would not be the truth. Within a few months a violent storm over the publication of a book threatened its very existence. The circumstances in which *The Adventures of a Black Girl in Her Search for God* was written must be briefly recapitulated in order to understand the sequel. The Shaws, travelling in South Africa during the winter of 1931–2, were driving at high speed along a road at Knysna, Cape Province, when G.B.S. who was at the wheel, being unfamiliar with the mechanism of the car, placed his foot on the accelerator instead of the brake, turned to the left instead of the right, and after hurtling into the veldt finally succeeded in bringing the car to a standstill, but not before Mrs Shaw who was sitting in the back seat amid piles of luggage had been seriously injured. During the month of her slow recovery Bernard Shaw wrote the 17,000 words of the book.

The Adventures of a Black Girl has sometimes been regarded as a piece of clever buffoonery, a *jeu d'esprit* to while away hours of tedium. But was it? The moment was hardly one to indulge in tomfoolery. In consequence of an accident of which he was the cause, Bernard Shaw's wife to whom he was completely devoted had been brought to death's door. A man's instinct in such a plight is not to jest but to pray. If one may conjecture from the outcome, it was precisely prayer to which he had recourse. Shaw being what he was, however, his fierce intellect asserted itself as the days passed, and he felt impelled to subject his Deity to analysis. The result is a fantasy somewhat after the manner of Swift, in which the central figure of the girl roving from place to place and encountering all kinds of things and people *en route* forms the main thread of the plot. It is not improbable that the black girl—suggested, one supposes, by his surroundings—is an allegory of his own soul. Her journey in search of God leads her to the Bible, whereupon she proceeds to knock down and knock out with a knobkerry of keen and merciless Voltairian wit the manifestations of the Godhead to be found in the Sacred Books. The general character of the story is evident from the opening paragraph of a letter from the author in answer to one of expostulation from Dame Laurentia, who upon hearing of the theme had asked Shaw to indicate the lines he was following:

4. WHITEHALL COURT, LONDON, S.W.1
14 April 1932

'Your letter has given me a terrible fright. The story is absolutely blasphemous, as it goes beyond all the Churches and all the gods. I forgot all about you, or I should never have dared. It is about a negro girl converted by a missionary, who takes her conversion very seriously and demands where she is to find God. "Seek and ye shall find Him" is the only direction she gets; so off she goes through the forest on her search, with her knobkerrie in her hand. Her search is only too successful. She finds the god of Abraham, and the god of Job; and I regret to say she disposes of both with her knob-kerrie. She meets Ecclesiastes (Koheleth) the Preacher, who thinks that death reduces life to futility and warns her not to be righteous overmuch. She meets Micah, roaring like a dragon and denouncing the god of Abraham as a bloodthirsty imposter with his horrible sacrifices. She meets Pavlov, who assures her that there is no god, and that life is only a series of reflexes. She meets St Peter carrying a cathedral on his shoulders. On her rushing to beg him to take care, as the weight will break his back, he assures her that it is only a paper cathedral and goes off gaily with it; but presently several others come along with paper churches, mostly much smaller and uglier, who warn her against St Peter until they begin throwing stones at one another and she has to run away to escape the fusillade. . . .'

When the author reaches the New Testament and proceeds with iconoclastic hammer to smash the Cross to pieces, reverence forbids quotation, for the profanation of divine names and ideas becomes revolting and unbearable. Yet as Peter Quennell pointed out in the *New York Times* in 1957, although G.B.S. was fascinated by the idea of faith, he 'liked to adopt the attitude of a worldly agnostic fly dancing around the circumference of a doctrinal web, tentatively approaching, boldly touching a filament, then immediately spreading his wings and taking to flight.' There is surely not a little of G.B.S. himself in the old gentleman who, for all his rationalism, is acutely aware of the supernatural plucking at his elbow; and the exposition of Shaw's New Testament exegesis ends on a strange note:

'She presently comes to a villa with a garden, which a frightfully intelligent looking but wizened old gentleman is cultivating in a rather amateurish way. ('Voltaire' [in margin]) On hearing of her quest, he remonstrates with her for her audacity, and confesses that if someone told him that God was coming to pay him a visit he should hide in the nearest mousehole. Then he tells her the story of Jupiter and Semele. "Besides," he says, "you need not trouble to hunt for God: he is always at your elbow." This impresses her so much that she goes into the garden and helps the old gentleman to cultivate it until he dies and bequeaths it to her. . . .

'The truth is, dear Sister Laurentia [he concludes] I have finished with all these deities, who seem to me more or less grotesque signboards announcing that the Holy Ghost is lodged within, though It is there only as It is everywhere.' [At this point he has carefully altered the small i of the original "it" in both places to a capital.] . . . 'I do not cry "He saved others: himself he cannot save," which is a fair taunt to a magician; I should say rather to the jeering crowd "He tried to save you and you slew him; so now you can follow your pet Barabbas to the devil: only, as I am determined that you shall have no excuse in the hour of your ruin, I shall also point out the way to you, though you shall not catch me in your legal and ecclesiastical nets if I can help it."

'And so on and so forth.

'Perhaps I should not disturb the peace of Stanbrook with my turbulent spirit; but as I want you to go on praying for me I must in common honesty let you know what you are praying for. I have a vision of a novice innocently praying for that good man Bernard Shaw, and a scandalized Deity exclaiming "What! that old reprobate who lives at Whitehall Court, for whom purgatory is too good. Don't dare mention him in my presence."

'The fact is, I have such an unruly imagination that I had better change the subject. I did not feel that your election could be more than a nominal change; for you would boss the establishment if you were only the scullery maid; and now that you are Abbess I feel comforted because you wont have to wash dishes as well as boss; and I wish you a wilful dominating interfering managing sort of Prioress so that you may henceforth have as little to do as possible except keep people's souls clean, as you help to keep that of your erring and worldly

Brother Bernard

'P.S. Shall I send you the story or not? It is very irreverent and iconoclastic but I don't think *you* will think it fundamentally irreligious.'

She demanded to see the book.

119

Two things emerge from a study of this curious fantasy and the correspondence between its author and Dame Laurentia to which it gave rise: possibly they are simply two facets of the same thing. Beneath the surface flummery and flippancy one has to recognize the story's underlying seriousness, its acknowledgement of the reality and the accessibility of God. 'Mere agnosticism,' Shaw declares in the Epilogue, 'leads nowhere.' Many critics and none more convincingly than G. K. Chesterton have dwelt on Bernard Shaw the Puritan. To regard G.B.S. as 'an atheist' in the style of popular newspaper reports is, needless to say, sheer nonsense. He could not or would not, however, seek God in anything physical or symbolical. Even Christ Himself 'comes between' God and Shaw, not indeed as He ought, in the sense of a bridge between God and man, the Way, the Truth and the Life, but as an obstacle like some barbed-wire entanglement to be ruthlessly and impatiently removed at all costs. In his own chimerical deliverance of mankind from 'supernatural superstition' therefore, Bernard Shaw sweeps away that full insight of mind and heart in the holy Scriptures where man reads the symbols of his own inner life presented by virtue of the mysterious analogy of matter and spirit. The result is a book scintillating with wit and fancy, and utterly devoid of wisdom and true imagination. The heroine, having disposed of the Biblical 'series of gods' with her knobkerry, 'from the monster Bogey Man to the Father; then to the spirit without body, parts, nor passions', reaches the unconvincing definition that God is Love, at which point she gives up the search altogether and settles down no nearer the object of her quest at the end than at the beginning. The Irishman's opinion that God is nothing more solid and satisfactory than an eternal but as yet unfulfilled purpose—'He's not properly made and finished yet'—is hardly even a serious conjecture. It follows, therefore, that the outcome of all Shaw's repudiations and destructions is a lifeless abstraction, a God hopelessly negative and remote with no apprehensible qualities whatever.

The second thing that emerges is -that Bernard Shaw—like Milton and Bunyan in the same Puritan tradition—stoutly maintained that *The Black Girl* had been written as the result of inspiration, nor did he ever, apparently, cease to regard it otherwise than as directly inspired by the Almighty. 'I was inspired to write this tale when I was held up in Knysna for five weeks in the African summer and English winter of 1932. . . . And now the story being written, I proceed to speculate on what it means.' So runs the epilogue, bearing out its author's assertion written on the fly-leaf of the forty-two-page first proof of the book sent to Dame Laurentia:

An Inspiration
Which came in response to the prayers of the nuns
of Stanbrook Abbey
and
in particular
to the prayers of his dear Sister Laurentia
for
Bernard Shaw

He must have feared a violent reaction. Together with the printer's proof—at some point after 20 April came a little play in which G.B.S. gave free rein to his propensity for teasing; he presumably hoped that its obvious fun would edulcorate her asperities:

> *Scene. God's office in heaven. Morning.*
> *The Recording Angel is writing up his books.*
> *Gabriel moodling about rather worried.*
> *Portrait of Our Lady over the mantelpiece.*
> *God comes in.*

God: Morning, Gabriel. Morning, Reck. Anything urgent this morning? Any prayers to be attended to?

Gabriel: The Abbess of Stan—

God: Again!! What a bother that woman is! What does she want *now*?

Gabriel: It's about that fellow Shaw.

God: But I've answered her prayers about him. She and her nuns pestered me about him for months. What she can see in him I can't imagine. But to please her I gave him a first class job in his own line and smashed up his wife for a month to give him time to do it.

The R. Angel (looking up from his book): What job was that?

God: To get Jesus off the cross. They have kept my poor boy nailed up there for nineteen hundred years, and wont listen to a word he says: they just keep on gloating over his execution. Shaw hates executions and thinks there's a lot in what Jesus says. So when Laurentia . . .

The R. Angel: You mustn't call her Laurentia now. She's an Abbess.

God: I shall call her what I like. She and her nuns worried me to save Shaw's soul until I was tired of hearing the fellow's name. For their sakes I did him the great honor [*sic*] of selecting him for the Deposition. What more does the woman want?

Gabriel: She doesnt approve of your way of saving him.

God: Not approve! She wants to dictate my ways to me, does she? I'll teach her. Put her down for five minutes in purgatory.

The R. Angel: You can't do that. Stanbury's—I mean Stan*brook*'s—an important place. It wouldn't do.

Gabriel: You'd better let her have her way. She's a shocking nuisance with her Shaw, I know; but she has been a faithful servant . . .

God: Gabriel: how often have I told you that faithful servants are the worst of tyrants? By the way, has Shaw done the job?

Gabriel: She won't let him.

God: D——

The scene hastily closes in; and the rest of the Divine Utterance is lost.

The ruse was successful but deceptive. The dialogue of the play led Dame Laurentia to assume that Shaw was ready to defer to her wishes and withdraw the book in its proof-stage. She wrote to thank him:

3 May 1932

Dear Brother Bernard,

. . . I thank you from my heart for listening to me. I have read most of the book and I agree with many of your ideas, but if you had published it I could never have forgiven you.

. . . You shall have more prayers by way of reward! Perhaps you will be naughty enough to set more value on my very deep gratitude.

I have now been five months an Abbess, and I find it much less easy than being scullery-maid could be. There is nothing wrong with my nuns, in fact I believe them to be the best nuns in the world, and they are much too good to me. But they have to be fed and clothed and their home has to be kept in decent order on an income that was never sufficient and is now decreasing. I am not going to let this thought make me unhappy, but you will realize that the responsibility is heavy.

I simply cannot find words to thank you for your answer to my letter, but you *know* how grateful I am.

In all the ensuing correspondence, G.B.S. never deviated a hair's breadth from his original position. He stubbornly persisted in his claim. It is characteristic of many who sternly reject any notion of the divine inspiration of the Scriptures, to regard their own private visions and assumptions as being unassailable and infallible, and there is an exquisite irony in the fear Bernard Shaw later expresses of upsetting Dame Laurentia's faith, while heartily assuring her of the impregnability of his own. Yet all this notwithstanding, a careful study of their dispute over the book may raise in the reader's mind the pertinent question: did Dame Laurentia really get to grips with the main problem? She censured and upbraided him, as indeed she had just cause to do, but did she ever fully grasp his point of view?

By nature neither of a speculative nor metaphysical turn of mind, she saw in the product of Shaw's inspiration only a grotesque parody of the Christian truths she held most sacred. What may, however, have lain at the base of the misunderstanding is precisely the ambiguity of the word 'inspiration'. In the first letter he ever wrote to her on the subject of St Joan, Bernard Shaw had informed her that from the age of twenty-four he had 'proceeded to purely mystical assumptions'. Rightly or wrongly, all mystics insist on the reality of their spiritual experiences; Shaw was therefore following in the tradition when he doggedly reiterated his conviction that he wrote *The Black Girl* as the result of direct inspiration. In face of so profoundly earnest a man, who, according to Shane Leslie, his fellow-countryman, was fundamentally an *anima naturaliter Christiana*, one would hesitate to deny that during those hours of intense anxiety and prayer he may have experienced some genuine *tactus Dei*, the 'divine touch' between his soul and God so well known to the mystics. Although such an experience, a flash of contact or whatever one may choose to call it, may be found more frequently in contemplatives who have attained to an habitually advanced state of prayer, yet it does not of itself imply high sanctity, any more than did the charismatic gifts bestowed upon the Corinthians. At the risk of being accused of putting Saul among the prophets and Shaw among the mystics, one may add that a life of personal asceticism, such as he undoubtedly led, has ever formed the traditional preparation which predisposes the soul for apprehension of the infinite, the thinning of the flesh being one of the accepted means for diminishing the barriers and opening up the avenues of the soul to the light and breath of heaven.

Where then, and why, did Bernard Shaw fail? He failed because he attempted to analyze, record and draw conclusions from an experience which, if real, necessarily surpassed the limits of human understanding. According to theologians, such contacts with the supernatural usually leave some permanent effect in the soul far below the plane of consciousness. Words in such circumstances, even at best, can only be a kind of algebraic symbol, and the trouble usually arises, as it did in the case of *The Black Girl*, when the memory and inventive faculty of the human mind attempt an interpretation of the divine action. Those who have read them know how bewilderingly concrete, disconcerting and contradictory the revelations of saints can prove. The advice of that sanest and most profound of all spiritual theologians, St John of the Cross, is *No admitir*—reject them all, pay no attention to what are purely secondary matters which may easily lead to error and illusion.

No one was more keenly alive to the danger than Bernard Shaw himself. 'I cannot too often repeat,' he asserts in the Epilogue to *The Black Girl*, 'that I am as liable as anyone else to err in my interpretation, and that pioneer writers, like other pioneers, often mistake their destination as Columbus did. That is how they sometimes run away in pious horror from the conclusions to which their revelations manifestly lead. I hold, as firmly as St Thomas Aquinas, that all truths, ancient or modern, are divinely inspired; but I know by observation and intro-spection that the instrument on which the inspiring force plays may be a very faulty one, and may even end like Bunyan in the Holy War, by making the most ridiculous nonsense of his message.'

Upon analysis, the story in essence is at the root of almost all mystical writings. The quest for God is simply the *Via Negativa* of Dionysius the Areopagite or of the anonymous author of *The Cloud of Unknowing*. It represents the soul's search for him by a negative process, by a progressive abstraction from sense and sensible things. The notion of an anthropomorphic material form of God is cast away, and the soul finally endeavours to contemplate the Godhead in his pure Being in a spiritual manner wherein all its powers are gradually drawn up into a peaceful unity which recognizes, to quote the Areopagite, that 'the One which is beyond thought surpasses the apprehension of thought, and the Good which is beyond utterance surpasses the reach of words'. But whereas such a supreme mystic as St John of the Cross ever relies and insists upon the necessity and safeguard of dogma and the divine revelation of the Scriptures, Bernard Shaw, flouting all save his own infallible authority, inevitably mingled what-ever may have been real in his contact with God with his own desires, preconceived ideas, wrongheaded prejudices and lively fancy, and so ended precisely as he feared, 'by making the most ridiculous nonsense of his message'.

The effect of the book on Dame Laurentia is difficult to describe. To the end of her life she could hardly bring herself to mention it. The open rejection of our Lord's divinity and the mockery of the crucifix by one whom she had come to regard as a dear friend filled her with grief and indignation; she felt utterly crushed and humiliated. It was all too clear to her that while his public insults to all that Christians hold most sacred would of necessity make many enemies, the book might easily gain a mastery over young and impressionable minds attracted by its levity and unable to pierce below the surface to the sound under-lying ideas. In December 1932 Shaw sent her the book in its final form, with an inscription which goes to prove that her letters during the course of the year had been such as to indicate that if it were published, he would no longer be *persona grata* at Stanbrook. The inscription runs:

'Dear Sister Laurentia,
'This black girl has broken out in spite of everything.
'I was afraid to present myself at Stanbrook in September.
'Forgive me.

G. Bernard Shaw
14 December 1932'

Dame Laurentia at once wrote to reprove G.B.S. in no measured terms for his blasphemous book. He was on a world cruise, and her letter reached him only in Thailand. While still on the voyage he wrote a long and detailed reply in shorthand in his letter book. The sequel, contained in a letter from Shaw to Dame Laurentia, is best told by himself:

4, WHITEHALL COURT, LONDON S.W.1
29 June 1933

'I have a wretched tale to tell, and can only hope that you will laugh at it.

'I was ridiculously surprised at your reception of *The Black Girl* story, which I innocently took to be a valuable contribution to the purification of religion from horrible old Jewish superstitions; and even my callousness was pierced by finding that it had shocked and distressed you. On the ship going round the world I wrote you a long letter about it, but could not feel sure that it might not wound you again, and so tore it up.

'Then I wrote you another, with the same result, after a few days reflection. But at the third attempt I succeeded, or thought I did. It was a long letter; and as I had no typewriter to make it legible for you I wrote it in shorthand for the ship's stenographer to transcribe. Alas, you never received it; for the next thing that happened was a ludicrous catastrophe.

'On that ship were hundreds of foolish Canadian and American worshippers of my publicity. Publicity worship sets great store by relics. The notebook in which I had drafted your letter (and others) vanished from my deck chair; and the offer of a guinea to any steward who could find it for me had no result. Your letter is in the collection of some devoutly Shavian thief. Your only remedy is anathema and major excommunication like that which brought the Jackdaw of Rheims to its senses; and for this you are too kindhearted. Our consolation must be that the thief probably cannot read shorthand; and if he (or she) calls in an expert it cannot be published without infringing my copyright, of which offence certain former legal proceedings of mine have established a wholesome dread in America.

'I will not try to reproduce the letter: the moment has passed for that. Besides, I am afraid of upsetting your faith, which is still entangled in those old stories which unluckily got scribbled up on the Rock of Ages before you landed there. So I must go delicately with you, though you need have no such tenderness with me; for you can knock all the story books in the world into a cocked hat without shaking an iota of *my* faith.

'Now that I think of it, it was a venial sin to write me such a cruel letter, and I think you ought to impose on yourself the penance of reading *The Black Girl* once a month for a year. I have a sneaking hope that it might not seem so very wicked the tenth or eleventh time as you thought it at first. You must forgive its superficial levity. Why should the devil have all the fun as well as all the good tunes?'

It was typical of Shaw the intellectual aristocrat to overrate the intelligence of the average man: it is an unfortunate human failing to lick the jam and leave the powder. He expected his readers, many of whom were young and vulnerable, to recognize his determination to see truth face to face even though it should slay him, whereas all that most of them were likely to see and stop at was the frivolity and irresponsibility in which that determination was clothed. Nevertheless, he must have realized that he was at grips with something greater than mere intellectual power when he received Dame Laurentia's acknowledgement:

13 July 1933

'Dear Brother Bernard,[1]

'Thank you for your letter. The fate of the long one written at sea is very sad, but if it was on the lines of your last one I fear it would not have given me much satisfaction. The fact is our points of view are so different, that talking, or writing, round the subject can be of little use. The only way to comfort me would be for you to withdraw the Black Girl from circulation, and make a public act of reparation for the dishonour it does to Almighty God. I still have such faith in your greatness of mind and heart, as to believe you capable of such an act, and to ask of you what I should not dream of proposing to a small mind. Do suppress the book and retract its blasphemies, and so undo some of the mischief it has wrought. I ask you this first and foremost in the interests of your own soul. I have made myself in some sense responsible for that soul of yours, and I hate to see you dishonour it.

'I think you cannot realise how deeply you have outraged the feelings of those who, like myself, believe in God and in Our Lord's divinity. These things are not vital to you, but they are to millions, and there are things too sacred to be played with. If you had written against my father or mother, you would not expect to be forgiven or received with any favour until you had made amends. Let me implore you to do this one thing and withdraw the book, even if you cannot find in your heart to imitate St Augustine and so many great minds who have given their retractations [*sic*] to the world.

'You know how I value your friendship and how truly I have believed in you. Is this precious thing to be sacrificed to a book that is unworthy of you?

'Do not be angry with me for writing in this way, but let me still be able to sign myself your

Sister Laurentia'

In his next letter, Shaw's obvious desire to conciliate gives no place for all that to apology or atonement. Gone is the familiar

[1] Dame Laurentia's actual letter to G.B.S. has come to light since the publication of *In a Great Tradition* where only a rough draft, found among her papers, was quoted.

signature, yet there is a touching note of pleading and, as ever, the request for prayer which is the hall-mark of a truly humble man.

THE MALVERN HOTEL
GREAT MALVERN
24 July 1933

'Sister Laurentia,

'You are the most unreasonable woman I ever knew. You want me to go out and collect 100,000 sold copies of *The Black Girl*, which have all been read and the mischief, if any, done; and then you want me to announce publicly that my idea of God Almighty is the antivegetarian deity who, after trying to exterminate the human race by drowning it, was coaxed out of finishing the job by a gorgeous smell of roast meat. Laurentia: has it never occurred to you that I might possibly have a more exalted notion of divinity, and that I dont as a matter of fact believe that Noah's deity ever existed or ever could exist? How could it possibly comfort you if I declared that I believed in him? It would simply horrify you. I know much better than you what you really believe. You think you believe the eighth chapter of Genesis; and I know you dont: if you did I would never speak to you again. You think you believe that Micah, when he wrote the eighth verse of his sixth chapter, was a liar and a blasphemer; but I know that you agree heartily with Micah, and that if you caught one of your nuns offering rams and calves and her first-born (if she had one) as a sacrifice to Jehovah you would have her out of the convent and into the nearest lunatic asylum before she could say Hail, Mary. You think you are a better Catholic than I; but my view of the Bible is the view of the Fathers of the Church; and yours is that of a Belfast Protestant to whom the Bible is a fetish and religion entirely irrational. You think you believe that God did not know what he was about when he made me and inspired me to write *The Black Girl*. For what happened was that when my wife was ill in Africa God came to me and said "These women in Worcester plague me night and day with their prayers for you. What are you good for, anyhow?" So I said I could write a bit but was good for nothing else. God said then "Take your

129

pen and write what I shall put into your silly head." When I had done so, I told you about it, thinking that you would be pleased, as it was the answer to your prayers. But you were not pleased at all, and peremptorily forbade me to publish it. So I went to God and said "The Abbess is displeased." And God said "I am God; and I will not be trampled on by any Abbess that ever walked. Go and do as I have ordered you." . . . "Well" I said "I suppose I must publish the book if you are determined that I shall; but it will get me into trouble with the Abbess; for she is an obstinate unreasonable woman who will never let me take her out in my car; and there is no use your going to have a talk with her; for you might as well talk to the wall unless you let her have everything all her own way just as they taught it to her when she was a child." So I leave you to settle it with God and his Son as best you can; but you must go on praying for me, however surprising the result may be.

Your incorrigible

G. Bernard Shaw

'P.S. Cockerell's friend Sir Emery Walker made a good end on Saturday—was apparently mending comfortably when he just gave a couple of gulps and died. . . . Walker was a most amiable man; but he had lived his life; and it was time for him to die.

'And for me also; so do not be unkind to me.

'We are here in Malvern as usual for the Festival, though I have no play in the bill this year. There is a miracle play, *The Conversion of St Paul*, to which you should come with all your nuns.'

The above letter, like the book itself, shows the fastidious Manichee to whom animal flesh was abhorrent, so revolted by the sacrifices of the Old Testament as to be rendered completely blind to the idea of Divine education which underlies the whole history of the people of God. It seems hardly necessary to remark that Shaw was quite right to contrast the Deities of Noah, Job and Micah: he was quite wrong to look upon them as three different gods. He did not see the God of infinite mercy who, taking an incredibly stupid, obstinate and savage people just as

130

they were—He might have taken the intelligent and highly civilized Greeks or Chinese, but for our everlasting comfort did not—entered into fellowship and loving intercourse with them at different stages according to their several capacities, and patiently prepared them by slow degrees for the full spiritual revelation of the New Testament. Argument, however, as Dame Laurentia was well aware, would have been useless. She therefore ignored the missive and its implicit request to call on her as in past years. The correspondence between the two over *The Adventures of a Black Girl* had occupied sixteen months, and although G.B.S. paid his annual visit to Malvern, in his own words he never dared to show his face at Stanbrook. The deadlock might have continued indefinitely had not the Muse of Comedy happily intervened.

On 6 September 1934, Dame Laurentia kept her Golden Jubilee. To mark the event, Pope Pius XI sent her the Papal blessing, bestowing upon her at the same time the distinction of the *Bene Merenti* medal in recognition of her work for the Church. The decoration was presented after Pontifical High Mass by Archbishop Williams, a friend for whom she had the deepest veneration. In the course of a private conversation with the Archbishop on the same day, she told him of the breach in her friendship with Bernard Shaw, and asked his advice. Several influential friends had been urging her for some time to reconsider her attitude, and there were weighty reasons in favour of reconciliation. Acting upon the Archbishop's counsel, she despatched without further token the charming jubilee card designed by two members of the community and printed from a woodblock. It consisted of a buff-coloured folder bearing on the outer cover the text from 2 Corinthians often applied to St Laurence and so suited to his Stanbrook namesake: *Hilarem datorem diligit Deus*—God loves a cheerful giver. The initial letter of the green and red script enclosed a figure of the Saint clad in deacon's dalmatic distributing loaves of bread to the poor. The inner page was simply inscribed:

IN MEMORY OF SEPT. 6
1884–1934
DAME LAURENTIA McLACHLAN
ABBESS OF STANBROOK

When after some delay the card reached Bernard Shaw, he immediately received it as an announcement of her death, and promptly wrote a letter of condolence to the community. With what merriment the 'deceased' Abbess read it we cannot know, but she was deeply moved by its obvious sincerity. Nothing could have healed the feud more successfully.

4, WHITEHALL COURT, LONDON, S.W.1
3 October 1934

'To the Ladies of Stanbrook Abbey
    Worcester
'Dear Sisters,
    'Through some mislaying of my letters I have only just received the news of the death of Dame Laurentia McLachlan. I was in Malvern from the end of July until the 16th September; and I never passed through Stanbrook without a really heartfelt pang because I might not call and see her as of old. But I had no knowledge of the state of her health and no suspicion that I should never see her again in this world.
    'There was a time when I was in such grace with her that she asked you all to pray for me; and I valued your prayers quite sincerely. But we never know exactly how our prayers will be answered; and their effect on me was that when my wife was lying dangerously ill in Africa through an accident I wrote a little book which, to my grief, shocked Dame Laurentia so deeply that I did not dare to show my face at the Abbey until I was forgiven. She has, I am sure, forgiven me now; but I wish she could tell me so. In the outside world from which you have escaped it is necessary to shock people violently to make them think seriously about religion; and my ways were too rough. But that was how I was inspired.
    'I have no right to your prayers; but if I should perhaps be remembered occasionally by those of you who remember my old visits I should be none the worse for them, and very grateful.

Faithfully

G. Bernard Shaw'

Next day he received a short note from his departed friend:

132

4 October 1934

'My dear Brother Bernard,

'As you see, I am not dead. I have only been keeping a Golden Jubilee in the habit, as we express it, and that little card was a souvenir of the event. At such a time my mind recalled old friends, you among them. . . . When next you are in the neighbourhood you must come and see me again, and I will tell you some of the wonderful ways in which my nuns honoured and delighted me on my Jubilee day. You might almost have heard echoes of it all in Malvern.

'You have my daily prayers. I hope they will have nothing but good results in future.

'Yours

Sr. Laurentia McLachlan'

Having committed what he described to Sydney Cockerell as 'a super howler', he had to extricate himself with grace, which he did in the following letter:

7 October 1934

'Laurentia! Alive!!

'Well!!!!!

'Is this a way to trifle with a man's most sacred feelings?

'I cannot express myself. I renounce all the beliefs I have left. I thought you were in heaven, happy and blessed. And you were only laughing at me! It is your revenge for that Black Girl.

'Oh, Laurentia, Laurentia, Laurentia, how *could* you.

'I weep tears of blood.

'Poor Brother Bernard'

For two years, and those the years following upon her election as Abbess, Dame Laurentia's letters had been stern, and had made no secret of the deep displeasure to which her decided action had borne witness. She had given indubitable proof—and was to give it again—that it was friendship, not adulation she had to offer. It is a tribute to Bernard Shaw's regard for her as well as to his essential greatness and humility, that when the storm had subsided, their friendship was resumed with all the old esteem and an ever-deepening veneration.

Within a few weeks of the reconciliation he was taking immediate steps to protect the inviolability of her enclosure and shelter her name from publicity. Towards the end of 1934, a certain lecturer circulated a rumour that as a result of a protest from the Abbess of Stanbrook, Bernard Shaw had decided to cut out parts of the Epilogue to *St Joan* in a revised edition. Dame Laurentia was of the opinion that the Epilogue contained the very pith of the play and had agreed with the author when, in defiance of those who persisted that it spoilt the drama, he had stated his resolute determination not to alter a word of it. The stupid untruth, however, was reported first in an English weekly newspaper, repeated a few days later in a Worcester paper, appeared in the *Osservatore Romano* of 7 and 8 January 1935, with slightly heightened emphasis, and finally found its way into the South African *Southern Cross*. Dame Laurentia at once feared that Bernard Shaw would break out into a denial which would call attention to her in a still more public manner, and wrote to him in haste to beg him to respect her wish to avoid press notices. 'I am not sure whether the Pope will think I deserve the Inquisition or another gold medal!' she ruefully remarked. It has been constantly objected against G.B.S. that he was an inveterate self-advertiser and never so happy as when in the limelight. Of the playwright so often in the public eye that may or may not have been true: of the friend with quick and lasting loyalties it was utterly false. By return of post he explained his ignorance of the press reports and demonstrated his promptitude in action when friendship demanded it.

25 January 1935

'Dear Sister Laurentia,

'Sacrilege! I am horrified. I know of course, that any public contradiction would just increase the publicity a hundredfold; and it is the publicity that is such an abominable desecration of your seclusion. But . . . I must stop him if I can. I have failed to find either his address or that of the Catholic Poetry Society. I am therefore writing to the Mother Superior of the Dominican Convent asking her to give me Mr ———'s address. If I can get it I will write a private letter to him and will, I hope, prevent his repeating the story in the course of his lectures. I will keep you *au courant*.

'The cruises are off. On the 24th November I dropped down dead. A few minutes later my too officious heart resumed its beat. I slept for three days and stayed in bed for a week afterwards. You see, I was simply tired. But I had no sooner recovered when my wife entered on a quite serious illness; and though she is no longer "in danger" as they say, the house is still full of doctors and nurses.'

From that moment newspaper reports automatically ceased and he saw to it that their names were never again associated in public.

In her letter acquainting him with the current rumours, Dame Laurentia had made enquiries about his latest book. He forthwith sent her an unpublished proof of *The Simpleton of the Unexpected Isles*, inscribed 'To Sister Laurentia from her erring Brother Bernard, 25 January 1935', with the remark: 'Since you ask about my latest play I risk the last remnant of your regard for me by sending you a copy. If only you can get over the first shock of its profanity you may find some tiny spark of divinity in it. You may ask why I write such things. I dont know: I have to. The devil has me by one hand and the Blessed Virgin by the other.'

It was barely three months since their mutual peace treaty, yet she straightway rose again to the attack with an undiminished energy which gave proof that she was not prepared to yield a single inch of the ground on which her feet were so firmly planted. It is generally admitted that Bernard Shaw had completed his finest and really enduring work prior to 1930: few of his friends can have told him so in language so forthright and unmistakable as the following:

7 February 1935

'I have been waiting till I could write at leisure about your letter and *The Simpleton*. You are quite right in believing that I should discover divinity under the profanity, and with very much I am in full sympathy, and heartily amused. Is it necessary though to be so offensively profane when satirizing vice and the British Empire? Need you use words of Scripture? It seems to me you could be quite as convincing without wounding the reasonable susceptibilities of those who believe in God with their whole hearts as I suspect you yourself do. I see the play is unpublished and I hope it will remain so, for I cannot believe you would do right in releasing it as it is. Whatever happens you absolutely must omit the allusion to the Immaculate Mother on p. 12. You know, as well as I do, that we do not worship her as God.

'It is annoying that when you could do and have done so much that is splendid you should devote yourself now to such mischievous things. I *do* ask you why you do such things and you have given me the answer that you *have* to. Don't you think the devil has had a good innings and that the Blessed Virgin might be given a turn? I simply hate to think after all the fine stuff you have written that these later things should appear. However you may parody the Day of Judgement you know the particular one for each of us can't be very far off and, my dear Brother Bernard, you will not be able to plead ignorance as the excuse of the evil that your books may do. You surely don't want to supply the devil with ammunition. But this you do by producing what might be harmless to strong minds but is almost certainly dangerous for weak ones. It makes me think of the danger of stupid people reading St Thomas Aquinas. They carry away with them all sorts of heresies propounded by him in his objections and forget his clear statements of dogma. Well, what about saying a Hail Mary (do you know it?) and asking Our Lady to take you by *both* hands? You would never regret it, I assure you, and she would hand you over to her Son who has the answer to all riddles, and who asks us to be like little children with regard to God. You know you have my daily prayers and I am sure you are aware that the end of such prayers is that you should be gathered into "the unity of all living souls in the Catholic Kingdom of God and His Church".'

His reply was hardly a defence so much as a remarkable self-revelation. With the skill born of lifelong controversy, he carried the war straight into the opposing camp and with characteristic audacity accused the Abbess of Stanbrook of being both unspiritual and anti-Catholic. He next proceeded to argue the claims of our Lady of Everywhere versus our Lady of Somewhere in a thesis by no means so extravagant as may appear at first sight. For there are deep affinities underlying all the great religions of mankind, and while in other systems there is a mixture of truth and error there is also a foreshadowing of the historical revelation of Christianity. Bernard Shaw was consequently right in recognizing in the Oriental shrines the Woman who stands at the very heart of the world. But one cannot help a suspicion that he was tinged with the ancient heresy that would have made her not merely Mother of God (which he does not seem to admit) but actually divine—one more Person to the Godhead. Or does he look upon her as just another way of regarding God as Mother and not Father? The ancient symbol of the Mother has various shapes and forms in various times and places, whether in the Syrian Mother-Goddess Astarte, the Egyptian Isis, the Greek Demeter, the Ephesian Artemis or the Latin Ceres. It might seem, on the surface, as if Christianity had simply supplied the figure of our Lady as another such divine personification of motherhood. Here, however, a necessary distinction between truth and error has to be drawn; it would appear from his letter as if Bernard Shaw had never worked out the implications of his theory. As Dame Laurentia pointed out to him in her strictures on *The Simpleton*, Mary is in no sense divine; even though truly the Mother of God she is a purely human creature. In virtue of her divine motherhood, she is the mightiest and most universal power in heaven and on earth, outside the Three Divine Persons of the Blessed Trinity, but she remains 'outside'. If motherhood is predicated of the Godhead at all, it is of her divine Son that it is predicated. Bernard Shaw's observations on the inadequacy of Western pictures and images of our Lady are pertinent enough. His own artless self-portrait, standing in reverential awe before an image of the Jains rapt 'into an ecstasy of prayer and trance of peace' with the salutation 'Hallo, Mary!' on his lips, has found no place —and it surely deserves a permanent one—in the Shavian iconography. The letter leaves one last query in the reader's mind. Was his worship of our Lady possibly the natural revenge of all the human feelings he so ruthlessly tried to eliminate from his consideration of God? Whatever the key to the riddle, at least his avowal undeniably breathes a pure and sublime veneration for her who is, 'Lo here! lo there!—ah me, lo everywhere!'

UNION-CASTLE LINE
M.V. "LLANGIBBY CASTLE"
12 April 1935

'On the Equator. 82° in the shade. On the east coast of Africa.
'Cara Sorella Laurentia,

'You are a puzzle to me with your unexpected rages. I ask myself, since I know that one becomes eminent in the Church through capacity for business more easily than by capacity for religion, "Can Laurentia be a completely irreligious (or areligious) managing woman who becomes boss in a convent exactly as she would become boss in a castle or in a laundry?"

'McLachlan? That suggests a clan of Covenanters to whom the worship of the B.V.M. is a damnable idolatry to be wiped out with claymore and faggot. Has Laurentia got that in her blood? If not, why in the name of all the saints does she fly out at me when I devoutly insist that the Godhead must contain the Mother as well as the Father?

'Or is it merely personal? So many women hate their mothers (serve them right, mostly!) and see red when the cult of maternity arises.

'You want me, as if it were a sort of penance, to say a lot of Hail Maries. But I am always saying Hail, Mary! on my travels. Of course I dont say it in that artificial form which means nothing. I say it in my own natural and sincere way when She turns up in the temples and tombs of Egypt and among the gods of Hindustan—Hallo, Mary! For you really cannot get away from Her. She has many names in the guide books, and many disguises. But She never takes me in. She favors Brother Bernardo with special revelations, and smiles at his delighted "Hallo, Mary!" When I write a play like *The Simpleton* and have to deal with divinity in it She jogs my elbow at the right moment and whispers "Now Brother B. dont forget *me*." And I dont.

'But then you come along in a fury and cry "How dare you? Cut all this stuff out, and say fifty Hail Maries."

'Which am I to obey? Our Lady of Stanbrook or Our Lady of Everywhere?

'When you are old, as I am, these things will clear up and become real to you. I wonder whether, if Raphael had lived

to be old like Michael Angelo, he would have given us something less absurd than the highly respectable Italian farmers'
daughters he imposed so smugly on the world as visions of the
B.V.M. Never have I stood before one of his Madonnas and
exclaimed Hallo, Mary! Raphael made the adoration of the
Mother impossible; but his view was so frankly and nicely
human and fleshly and kindly that in the Dresden Madonna
he produced for all time the ideal wet nurse, healthy, comely,
and completely brainless.

'On the other hand there is the giantess-goddess of Cimabue
with her magnetic stare, a much deeper conception, but with
just a little too much of the image and too little reality to be as
approachable as the Egyptian goddesses of the great period.

'In short, the Christian Maries are all failures. This suggests
that the Jains were right in excluding God from their ritual
as beyond human power to conceive or portray. At least that
is their theory; but in practice they have in their shrines images
of extraordinary beauty and purity of design who throw you
into an ecstasy of prayer and a trance of peace when they look
at you, as no Christian iconography can.

'I said to the pundit who showed me round "Those images
are surely gods, are they not?" "Not at all," he said, "they are
statues of certain very wise men of the Jains." This was obvious
nonsense; so I pointed out that a man kneeling in the shrine
(having first washed himself from head to foot) was clearly
praying to a god. "Pooh!" said the pundit with enormous
contempt, "he is only a heathen idolator."

'It is in these temples that you escape from the frightful
parochiality of our little sects of Protestants and Catholics, and
recognize the idea of God everywhere, and understand how
the people who struggled hardest to establish the unity of God
made the greatest number of fantastically different images of
it, producing on us the effect of a crude polytheism.

'Then comes the effort to humanize these images. The
archaic Minerva becomes the very handsome and natural
Venus of Milo. The Cimabue colossus becomes the wet nurse.
Bellini's favorite [sic] model becomes as well known to us in her
blue hood as any popular actress. Leonardo, Michael Angelo,
Correggio (once, in the dome in Parma) lift these leading

ladies, these stars of the studio, for a moment out of the hopelessly common; but on the whole, wisdom is with the Jains.

'I have been getting into trouble by backing up a proposal to give Christ's Cathedral in Dublin to the Catholics, leaving St Patrick's to the Protestants. The two cathedrals are in a poor neighbourhood within a stone's throw of one another. St Patrick's was restored by Guinness the brewer, Christ's by Roe the distiller. The drunkenness of the poor Catholics paid for both: why should they not have at least one?

'But my individual opinion is that cathedrals should be for all men, and not for this or that sect.

'By this time we have passed the equator, and it is time for me to stop blaspheming.

'Bless you, dear Laurentia.

G. Bernard Shaw'

Their second duel left not the slighest trace of resentment on either side. Within a few months Dame Laurentia, who had been very ill that year, was welcoming G.B.S. at Stanbrook and giving proof once more of how much she valued 'the friendship of this great and dear man', as she put it. On his part, the letter he wrote just after his visit in August 1935 suggests in its air of gay insouciance something of their mutual sympathy and complete understanding:

MALVERN, *30 August 1935*

'Dearest Sister Laurentia,

'You cannot imagine how delighted I was to find you shining in all your old radiance before the cloud of illness came upon you. If ever I write an opera libretto, it will be rather like *Die Zauberflöte*; but I shall call it *The Merry Abbess*.

'As I drove back here it was a magically lovely evening, or seemed so to me. I felt ever so much the better for your blessing. There are some people who, like Judas Iscariot, have to be damned as a matter of heavenly business; . . but if I try to sneak into paradise behind you they will be too glad to see you to notice me . . .

'I promised to send that handsome young Dom Basil a book,

and have actually bought it for him; but for the moment I have mislaid the address he gave me. It will turn up presently.

Always your

Brother Bernard'

With this letter he sent her an unpublished rough proof of *The Millionairess*, bearing the inscription:

'Dear Sister Laurentia,

'This is one of my entirely profane works; so you must read it in an unprofessional spirit.

Brother Bernard.

Malvern *30 August 1935*'

Her acknowledgement gives some indication of the understanding that lay deep and unruffled beneath the stormy surface of an occasional confrontation between the two protagonists:

9 September 1935

'My dear Brother Bernard,

'Many thanks for your nice letter (useful word "nice", if a little overworked), and the new play, which entertained me enormously. The "dirty question of money", to use Dom Basil's phrase, is beautifully castigated, and I am more glad than ever not to have a millionairess in my monastic family, useful as her cash would be.

'"The Merry Abbess" would draw well! You'll send me a copy, I know.

'It was a really big pleasure to have a talk with you. As to where you go eventually, that depends entirely on you, and you would be wise to choose Heaven. People are not sent to Hell, they go there because they choose that fate. When people talk of going there, it is sometimes a way of giving themselves leave to do as they like, just as when Catholics say they have lost their faith it nearly always means they have lost their morals. Anyhow, *you* are not going to the wrong place if I can do anything to prevent it! So, again, God bless you.

'Yours devotedly

Sister Laurentia'

141

He continued to make her gifts of autographed unpublished proofs, and from this time onwards his always vivacious letters are pervaded with an attractive note of gentle serenity. In 1944 he sent his latest publication, *Everybody's Political What's What?* with the following letter written on the title-page:

AYOT SAINT LAWRENCE
4 September 1944

'I hope this will not arrive late for your Diamond Jubilee tomorrow. It is too late for mine by twenty years: I was eightyeight last month but one. The saint who called me to the religious life when I was eighteen was Shelley.

'But you have lived the religious life: I have only talked and written about it.

'You ask me how I am. I must reply, the better for your prayers; for, deaf, and doddering and dotty as I inevitably am at my age, I am astonishingly well, much weller than I was a year ago.

'Look at my portrait: it was taken this year. You would still know me if you met me. I wish you could. I count my days at Stanbrook among my happiest.

G. Bernard Shaw'

The letter leaves no doubt as to the writer's sincerity: facile compliments did not flow easily from Shaw's lips or pen. That Dame Laurentia was not foolishly flattered is obvious, for her serious reply contains a veiled challenge:

19 September 1944

'My dear Brother Bernard,

'Among the many pleasant and valued contents of my postbag on the 6th there was none more valued or more welcome than your letter and book. Thank you very much for both. It is good to know that age scarcely counts for you. The book (into which I have only dipped but which I look forward to reading) shews that the old verve is undamaged.

'Sixty years of enclosed life leaves me happier than ever for having chosen this path—though, as Tagore sang: "We cannot *choose* the best. The Best chooses us." If people only knew the freedom of an enclosed nun! I believe you can understand it better than most people and I only wish we shared the faith that is its foundation. I never forget you in my prayers nor fail to commend you to our Lady. Your lovely reliquary with its stone from Bethlehem is treasured.

'Again my best thanks
Sr. Laurentia McLachlan OSB, Abbess'

G.B.S. kept his ninetieth birthday on 26 July 1946 and four days later in the same bold if somewhat tremulous hand wrote to acknowledge her birthday greetings:

'Dear Sister Laurentia,
'For the past week I have had over 100 congratulations a day. But for two strong men who have worked hard tearing them up for me I should never have been 90. Saving your reverence I do not give a damn for congratulations. But prayers touch me and help me. It is good for me to be touched. Stanbrook prayers must have some special charm; for I never forget them.
'On the birthday I had a word with Cockerell. He is beginning to look a bit oldish: but he can walk without a stick, which I dare not attempt, as the police would charge me with being drunk and incapable. However, I am quite happy in my garden, where the weeks race past like minutes: their speed is incredible. I can still write a bit, and have plenty to do. . . .'

Prayer had invariably loomed large in his correspondence with Dame Laurentia. Never did he make such a simple and open profession of faith in its efficacy, however, as in a long letter typewritten by himself with frequent corrections in ink and here reproduced in its entirety by kind permission of Mr Tunney himself:

17 August 1948

'Beloved Sister Laurentia,
'Just as your letter came it happened that I had a visit from another very special friend whose vocation was as widely different from yours as any two vocations on earth can be, and yet who is connected in my thoughts with your subject, the efficacy of prayer. He is Gene Tunney, an Irish American, still

143

famous as the undefeated Heavy Weight Boxing Champion of the World, no less.

'He is a good man all through, and entirely presentable in any society.

'He comes of a devout Catholic family, pillars of The Church; but, as he put it, "When I went into the ring as a professional I dropped all that." But though he dropped the faith it did not drop him. He made a fortune by his fights and when he retired he married a rich woman. The young couple came travelling to Europe, and found themselves in a pleasure island in the Adriatic, where I met him and made friends with him. He told me what had just happened to him. His young wife was attacked by the very rare complaint, unknown to most surgeons, of a double appendicitis. Nothing but a major operation could save her; and there was on the island only one old and useless doctor. Death within ten hours was certain. Gene, helpless and desperate, could only watch her die. Except one thing, to go back to his faith and pray. He prayed.

'Next morning very early there landed in the island the most skilful surgeon in Germany, the discoverer of double appendices. Before ten o'clock Mrs Tunney was out of danger and is now the healthy mother of four children.

'Protestants and sceptics generally see nothing in this but a coincidence; but even one coincidence is improbable, and a bundle of them as in this case hardly credible in a world full of miracles. The prayer, the timing of the surgeon's arrival, his specialization for the rare disease, were so complicatedly coincidental that if they had been reported to me from China about strangers I should not have believed the story. As it is I do not doubt it; and it goes to confirm the value I instinctively set on your prayers. So do not forget me in them. I cannot explain how or why I am the better for them; but I like them and am certainly not the worse.

'Perhaps I have told you the Tunney story before; for old men repeat their old stories mercilessly. No matter: it will bear twice telling.

'I am so very old (92) that you would hardly know me if I could now get as far as Stanbrook. I am very groggy on my legs, and make blunders by the dozen; but I have passed the second childhood that comes at 80 or thereabouts; and got that clear second wind that follows it; so that though my body is going to bits, the latest born scrap of my soul still marches on.

'I send you a private copy of a trivial comedy [*Buoyant Billions*] which is the best I can now do. It will interest you only as everything interests you; for though you are an enclosed nun you have not an enclosed mind, as so many women at large have.

'Do not for a moment feel bound to answer this: you have no time for duty letters. A hail on my next birthday, if it ever arrives, will satisfy me.

G. Bernard Shaw'

Two more letters marked the two remaining years of his life, and each brought its repeated profession of faith. In 1949 he typed and made necessary corrections in the following letter, in which prayer is again the recurrent theme:

2 September 1949

'Dearest Sister Laurentia,

'I got your letter on my 93rd birthday: the only one that was not hurried into an overloaded waste basket with very unseemly objurgations.

'So many people in Ireland kept sending me . . . presents that many of them could ill afford, that I had to declare publicly that I needed nothing that money could buy, and asked only for their unpurchasable prayers. Since then I have been so overwhelmed with prayers that I am in danger of my Eternal Judge exclaiming "Damn this fellow that I am being pestered about: to hell with him." I get piles of medals of the Blessed Virgin, with instructions that if I say a novena she will give me any help I ask from her; and I have to reply that we are in this wicked world to help her and not to beg from her.

'For some inexplicable spiritual reason I put Stanbrook prayers into a class by themselves, and have no fear of their getting on heavenly nerves. . . . I am horribly old (93) and cannot walk much. Happily my wits are livelier than my legs; but I cannot in the course of nature last much longer. Cockerell turns up occasionally; and we correspond quite often.

'Do not dream of having to answer this: it is only to let you know that I am still faithful, though Stanbrook is too far for me to travel.

G. Bernard Shaw'

These yearly letters touched Dame Laurentia deeply. 'He is faithful and kind,' she remarked, 'and I think it wonderful of him to find time for me. It is certainly a proof of that sincerity which so many people doubt his possessing.' On his ninety-fourth and last birthday she wrote as usual to tell him that the community would offer special prayers for him that day. She received in return an amusing account of the incessant telephone calls, the armies of photographers and reporters, the deliveries of giant cakes, letters and telegrams which had kept him in a state of siege all day. At the close of the letter he uttered his last gracious *Ave atque vale*: 'God must be tired of all these prayers for this fellow Shaw whom He doesn't half like. He has promised His servant Laurentia that He will do His best for him, and we had better leave it at that. The thought of Stanbrook is a delight to me. It is one of my holy places.'

With her last tranquil farewell, she sent him as she had sent Canon Wilson twenty years earlier, a lavender-bag with its evocative scent of high summer and the festival of her patron St Laurence:

8 August 1950

'My dear Brother Bernard,
'We both live under the patronage of St Laurence, so I send you a little token for his feast-day. The lavender harvest has just come in and one of my jobs is to pack it into little bags for our sale of work. You will accept it as thanks for the very kind and unexpected letter you wrote me, and I hope the fragrance will keep you in mind of Stanbrook where you are so affectionately remembered. There is a little medal of our Lady buried in the lavender, but you will not object to that.
'This requires no acknowledgement.

Sr. Laurentia'

He died a few months later at dawn on the morning of All

Souls' Day, 2 November 1950—a day set apart by official pro-
clamation as one of solemn intercession:

'On this day the commemoration of all the faithful departed;
on which day Holy Church . . . strives to help those who still
suffer in Purgatory by her prayers which are of avail before
Christ her Lord and Bridegroom, in order that as speedily as
possible they may join the society of the citizens on high.'

Bernard Shaw had asked one thing of the Stanbrook community and his fellow-countrymen: the gift of their unpurchasable prayers. That gift was now his in fullest measure. 'I can
never forget,' wrote Dame Laurentia to Sydney Cockerell the
same day, 'that it was through you that I gained the right of
calling him my friend. His fidelity to that friendship was always
a marvel to me. Dying on All Souls' Day he will have the prayers
of many.'

From morning until night there rose a steady stream of sup-
plication according to Catholic custom, in the dear formula of
the Rosary familiar from childhood: 'Holy Mary, Mother of God,
pray for us sinners now and at the hour of our death.'

'And Sion said: Can a mother forget her child, so as not to have
pity on the son of her womb?' (*Isa.* 49.15.)

'When I have to deal with divinity She jogs my elbow at the
right moment and whispers "Now Brother *B.* dont forget *me.*"
And I dont.' (G.B.S.)

Our Lady wears a crown in a strange country,
  The crown he gave,
But she has not forgotten to call to her old companions,
  To call and crave;
And to hear her calling a man might arise and thunder
  On the doors of the grave. (G.K.C.)

Within three years Dame Laurentia herself was dying. For
nearly seventy years she had sung, prayed, meditated, worked
and joyfully lived in the seclusion of her monastic cloister.
During the few days preceding her death, each nun saw her

alone, without any formality, rank or dramatic leave-taking. She made one exception in the case of a young nun on the eve of her solemn profession whom she bade a simple *au revoir* in characteristic monosyllables: 'Child, I am going to God. That is what I came for—what we all came for—to go to God. I am sorry I shall not be alive for your profession, but, Child, *I shall be there*. Give yourself wholly to God, to be entirely consecrated, sanctified, glorified.'

At a quarter past five on Sunday the 23rd of August 1953, as her nuns stole down in the grey morning light to chant God's praises, signed with the sign of the Cross, she drew a great, deep breath and slept in peace.

*   *   *   *   *

Index